ADRIFT IN MELBOURNE

ALSO BY ROBYN ANNEAR

Bearbrass: Imagining early Melbourne

Nothing But Gold: The diggers of 1852

The Man Who Lost Himself:
The unbelievable story of the Tichborne Claimant

Fly a Rebel Flag: The Eureka Stockade

A City Lost and Found: Whelan the Wrecker's Melbourne

Nothing New: A history of second-hand

ADRIFT IN MELBOURNE

SEVEN WALKS WITH ROBYN ANNEAR

TEXT PUBLISHING MELBOURNE AUSTRALIA

The Text Publishing Company acknowledges the Traditional Owners of the country on which we work, the Wurundjeri people of the Kulin Nation, and pays respect to their Elders past and present.

textpublishing.com.au

The Text Publishing Company
Wurundjeri Country, Level 6, Royal Bank Chambers, 287 Collins Street, Melbourne Victoria 3000 Australia

Published by The Text Publishing Company, 2021

Cover design by Chong W.H.
Cover photograph *'Paris end' of Collins Street*, 1958 [picture] / Mark Strizic from State Library of Victoria
Maps and illustrations by Simon Barnard
Page design by Imogen Stubbs
Typeset in Adobe Garamond Pro by J&M Typesetting

Printed and bound in Australia by Griffin Press, part of Ovato, an accredited ISO/NZS 14001:2004 Environmental Management System printer.

ISBN: 9781922330970 (hardback)
ISBN: 9781922459206 (ebook)

A catalogue record for this book is available from the National Library of Australia.

FSC
www.fsc.org
MIX
Paper from responsible sources
FSC® C009448

This book is printed on paper certified against the Forest Stewardship Council® Standards. Griffin Press holds FSC chain-of-custody certification SGSHK-COC-005088. FSC promotes environmentally responsible, socially beneficial and economically viable management of the world's forests.

For Michael

CONTENTS

INTRODUCTION

The city is always vanishing, maybe never faster than now.

ALEXANDRA SCHWARTZ IN THE *NEW YORKER*, DECEMBER 2020

Vanished doesn't mean gone. In Melbourne—in any place—things change all the time. Yet, the way I see it, nothing's ever really gone.

Like other books of mine, this one deals largely in absences—of people, buildings, institutions and even lions that were here before us. Lately we've been absent too. But absence is no obstacle to memory. This book is proof.

Melbourne's original self-definition was 'not-Sydney'. If you ask me, it still does the job. Much of what's been said since in Melbourne's favour is mere puffery: 'Marvellous Melbourne' (travelogorrhoea); 'Paris of the Pacific' (*comme si*); 'World's Most Liveable City' (whatever); 'Laneway Melbourne' (pimped for Instagram).

So, call me an unfluencer. I make no special claims for Melbourne: only that it's the city I know best, having dug deep into it and walked it all over and over. Besides, I like the place.

This book is ostensibly a walking guide, but you can drift just as well from a couch. Armchair city-walkers can get their bearings using Google Maps and Street View.

Plus, there's a Melbourne mobility map online (or in any Melways) showing the relative steepness of the city streets, so you can chart how much legwork you're missing out on.

If you do find yourself afoot in the city with this book, be sure to look up from the page—up and around. Just because the places you'll read about have mostly disappeared doesn't mean there's nothing to see. One Sunday morning in La Trobe Street I spotted a ghost ship riding high on a west-facing wall, its uncanny square-rigged sails formed by reflected sunlight from windows in the building opposite. Walking in the city, something is sure to snag your interest; when it does, try not to Google it straightaway but let yourself wonder a while. Wondering will take you places Google can't.

If nothing's ever really gone, then let's acknowledge the story that underlies all the places in this book: the dispossession of Indigenous people and desecration of their culture. By *underlies*, I don't mean figuratively. Melbourne is built on land seized from its traditional custodians, sometimes with deadly force. When we focus on the city's history, *that* foundational and enduring fact tends to get overwritten, forgotten. Let's remember it. And let's consider, too, what stories—what memories—must have attached to this place in all the time that came before. More than we'll ever know.

EXPLORE FURTHER ONLINE

Whether reading at home or on the move, you'll want to see pictures of some of the disappeared places and people mentioned in this book. Start with the State Library Victoria website, where you'll find Melbourne's digitised visual past—photographs, maps and more. Other repositories of Melbourne images online include the Royal Historical Society of Victoria, Public Records Office Victoria, the City of Melbourne's Art and Heritage Collection and the Victorian Parliamentary Library.

As a vivid illustration of the changing city, you can't beat *https://1945.Melbourne* which pulls off a neat time-travel trick by overlaying a 1945 aerial photo of Melbourne with one from 2015. Zoom in on the CBD, 'slide' the recent image across the old black-and-white one and you get to see the low-rise city transformed, block by block.

The website www.emelbourne.net.au hosts a wealth of Melbourne history. The entire contents of the *Encyclopedia of Melbourne* can be found there. Comprehensively indexed, with clickable links, it's your readiest source of further information about places, people and events touched on in this book.

Also at the eMelbourne website you can explore decades' worth of old Melbourne directories (1857–80), digitised and searchable. For a granular snapshot of a lost (yet familiar) Melbourne, browse the occupants of any street or lane in a given year. Trust me, it'll change the way you see the city.

WALK 1

WALTZ IN SIX LESSONS

In which we encounter women tight-laced,
in pieces and seeking a place to sit down

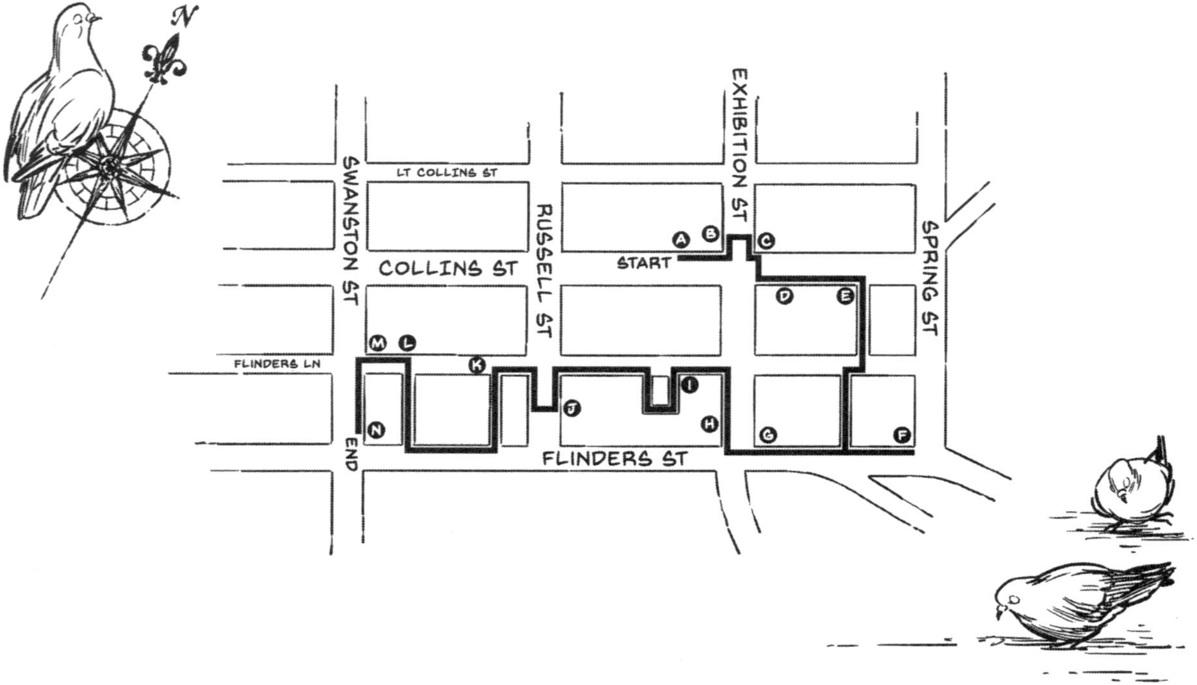
N
SPRING ST
EXHIBITION ST
RUSSELL ST
SWANSTON ST
LT COLLINS ST
COLLINS ST
FLINDERS LN
FLINDERS ST
START
END
A
B
C
D
E
F
G
H
I
J
K
L
M
N

1:A

LE LOUVRE
74 COLLINS STREET

This three-storey building is a sprig of parsley: a garnish to the tower that overshadows Collins Street. Number 74 survives as an early example of the townhouses that used to line this end of Collins Street, albeit one so altered over the course of 165 years that its only original interior feature is the staircase.

For many decades it served as a doctor's rooms and residence, then in 1927 its front wall was knocked through for shop windows. In the 1970s, upping the demolition ante, its neighbours were amputated to falsify a Collins Street address for the towering Nauru House (behind, facing Exhibition Street), leaving exposed a roughcast party wall. Number 74 would have gone too, if its owner had been willing to sell.

From 1934 to 2010 this was Le Louvre, a fashion salon so exclusive that few Melburnians ever stepped over the threshold. Its copper-framed windows were dressed with gauzy curtains that repelled the plebeian gaze, so when Le Louvre finally sold up and a high-end hipster brand moved in, it was a shock to see inside. Disappointing, too. It was just another shop, after all. Except for that staircase, leading upstairs…to what?

The building's first occupant, in 1855, was Thiennette Bérigny, a homeopathic physician from France via New Orleans. Downstairs was his dispensary, where he specialised in the treatment of addiction to mainstream medicines. Upstairs, his wife Adèle gave birth to two sons, and the doctor held regular séances. This was nothing out of the ordinary. Spiritualism was everywhere at that time, and in Melbourne, this stretch of Collins Street was its hub. It was contact with spirit guides at Dr Bérigny's séance circle that led William Terry to found the Victorian Spiritualists' Union (still in existence) and to open a 'spiritualistic and freethought' bookshop and herbal emporium in Russell Street, where, for years, the Theosophical Society had its rooms.

Six doors down from Bérigny's, towards Alfred Place, lived Dr James Motherwell. A leading light on the Melbourne medical scene who trained homegrown doctors at the university, Motherwell was also a proponent of phrenology and animal magnetism, and for many years hosted his own influential spiritualist circle. It was there that, in his teens, future prime minister Alfred Deakin contacted the spirit of John Bunyan, under whose influence he composed a sequel to *The Pilgrim's Progress*. Between Motherwell's and Bérigny's lived Dr Richard Youl who, as Melbourne's coroner for forty years, had his own way of dealing with the dead.

And in that gap beside Number 74, for almost a hundred years, stood Ogg's chemist shop. Its ornate cast-iron verandah, originally one of many along Collins Street, was the last to be pulled down. The city council considered the old-fashioned pillar verandahs an eyesore, as well as a car-parking hazard, and ordered them all removed before the Royal Visit of 1954. Preservationists and pedestrians pleaded for Ogg's verandah: not only was it old and stately, it offered shelter from the weather on this exposed stretch of Collins Street. But in vain. During the Queen's visit, the *Illustrated London News* ran a feature on Melbourne's architectural gems, highlighting—too late—Ogg's verandah and its 'sophisticated urban air'.

When I was an office girl of eighteen, post-pantyhose revolution, some perverse retro impulse made me try wearing stockings and suspenders. Getting off the bus in Collins Street of a morning, I'd feel the *ping!* of stockings popping off their suspenders and would have to shuffle, knees together, to a sheltering doorway so I could hitch up my skirt and re-couple. One time, mid-manoeuvre, the facing door opened—was it Le Louvre?—and a chic matron raked me with the kind of look usually reserved for vermin. It spelled the end of me and stockings.

1:B

DUVALLI'S DANCING ACADEMY
75 EXHIBITION STREET

A building that once stood here was occupied in the 1880s by Duvalli's Dancing Academy. Heloise Duvalli was the elder of the dancing Duvalli sisters, who introduced to Australia the Parisian Quadrille—better known as the can-can. Ahead of their Adelaide season in 1879, the Duvallis were warned by the police against 'indecent dancing', to which the spirited Heloise replied that 'they would dance the can-can in spite of everything'. And, to the wowsers' dismay, they did.

With Heloise's husband, actor and ballet master Charles Coutts, the Duvalli sisters led their own vaudeville company of forty-odd artists, touring Europe and the US for a decade or more. When the company disbanded in 1880, Mr and Mme Coutts-Duvalli settled down here and opened a dance school. For a guinea, gentlemen and ladies were guaranteed waltz proficiency in just six lessons.

During its years on this spot, the dancing academy's address changed from Stephen Street to Exhibition Street. Stephen Street had long held the bedraggled reputation of saddling yard to the city's red-light quarter. In 1880 the epoch-making Melbourne International Exhibition opened in the purpose-built Exhibition Buildings in

Carlton Gardens. Stephen Street, the main approach, was renamed Exhibition Street and vigorous civic attempts were made to expunge the *déclassé*. Then followed years of awkward transition—'*formerly known as* Stephen Street', '*also known as* Exhibition Street'—before the paint finally dried on the new name around 1895.

By that time, the Coutts-Duvallis were gone, their dancing academy having lost its feet in the financial panic of 1893. They returned to the colonial touring circuit, this time with their daughters Rosalie and Claire as main attraction. Rosalie danced ballet and played the harp, while Claire (calling herself Heloise Austa) played piano and sang. Off-stage, Austa wrote occasional short stories—tales of rural pathos and redemption, mostly—for newspapers like the *Weekly Times*. In one titled 'Ella Drummond, Storyist', a newspaper editor meets one of his contributors (the 'storyist' of the title) and concludes that 'there are, perhaps, more heroines in real life than are ever recorded in the pages of fiction'.

1:C

OCCIDENTAL HOTEL
64 COLLINS STREET (CORNER OF EXHIBITION)

The stage-name 'Heloise Austa' was no doubt a patriotic tribute inspired by the Melbourne-born operatic soprano Dame Nellie Melba (real name: Helen Porter Mitchell). On this corner stood one of several city hotels that would claim Melba always stayed there when she was in town. Originally licensed in 1848, when Melbourne was still part of New South Wales, this was the first hotel at the east end of Collins Street, which was then still considered somewhat countrified. It would change its name several times before settling on the Occidental.

When the Olympics came to town in 1956, Melbourne suffered pangs of embarrassment over the seedy, outdated accommodation offered by even its leading hotels. There was scarcely an *en suite* to be had. The Occidental's licence came up for renewal that year and a hotel inspector found the hotel 'old-fashioned in many respects'. He didn't just mean the potted palms, stoneware hot-water bottles and narrow, twisting hallways; he saw dishes being washed in a tin tub outside the kitchen door and the bathrooms were unmentionable. Faced with demands to modernise, the Occidental instead gave up.

A writer in the *Sun* mourned the Occidental Hotel as 'one of the last links with a more leisurely, easy-going Melbourne when Australians were content to be themselves and the customs and decorative schemes of Honolulu and Las Vegas were not regarded as necessarily the high peak of civilisation'. (And the Southern Cross wasn't even built yet—see 4:V.) When newspapers published a sketch of the building that would replace the Occidental—a seven-storey office tower with a glass curtain wall—the artist Norman Lindsay, still up for trouble at age eighty, wrote to say:

> *This building, which will destroy Melbourne's most pleasing vista, is a final triumph to modernistic art, with its slogan of death to all beauty. There is only one finality to such abominable glass anthills and that is a bomb. Any old bomb will do, not necessarily atomic.*

For a couple of months in 1960, between demolition and redevelopment, the site was occupied by a novelty: probably the last *house* ever to be built in Collins Street (and the first in at least fifty years). A cream brick-veneer display home built practically overnight, it was open to the public as a charity fundraiser. And talk about 'the high peak of civilisation'—it had its own swimming pool!

1:D

ORIENTAL HOTEL

41–53 COLLINS STREET (COLLINS PLACE ENTRANCE)

With a fortune made from gold-dredging in north-east Victoria, Pearson Tewksbury started Melbourne's first motorised taxi service in 1910. When in town, he always stayed at the Melba-worthy Oriental Hotel, which stood on this spot. At least he did until his wife had a falling out with the manager. Tewksbury's solution was to *buy* the Oriental.

He spent lavishly during the 1920s to upgrade the hotel 'on the newest cosmopolitan lines'. A tireless traveller, Tewksbury never returned from abroad without a trunkful of ideas for improving his hotel—and the city. After a trip to Europe and the US in 1937 he railed against the licensing restrictions that prevented tourists in Melbourne getting a drink after six o'clock and made the city's hotels like 'morgues'. And he urged Melbourne to follow the lead of other international cities and get rid of its 'dreadful' trams. Collins Street was ruined, said Tewksbury, by such an 'antiquated' form of transport. He looked forward to a day when the clatter of trams would be heard at the Oriental no more.

After World War II, he drew up grand plans for a new Oriental, complete with air-conditioning and underground car parking. Still no *en suite* bathrooms—but all five hundred rooms would have beds that converted into couches and dressing tables that doubled as writing desks. Tewksbury predeceased Melbourne's trams, though, and his big plans for the Oriental fizzled out.

But one idea of his did come to fruition. Five years after his death, the Oriental's new owner introduced the sidewalk café to Melbourne, with nineteen tables, shaded by umbrellas, along the Collins Street kerbside. Tewksbury had mooted the idea as early as 1933. Given the chance, he said, Melburnians, like Parisians, would 'sit in the sunshine before their cafés and muse on life and art'. He did wonder, though, if they might be too self-conscious for outdoor dining.

He needn't have worried. Come 1958, the café was an instant hit, with customers lining up for espresso and sandwiches under the plane trees. In fact, demand for tables allowed no time for musing. The café was threatened with closure in 1960, when motorists complained that it interfered with parking. This was too much. The Oriental had already lost its signature cast-iron verandah, on the same bogus justification, in the verandah blitz of 1954. Besides, the centrepiece of a new tourism campaign pitching Melbourne as a cosmopolitan destination was—you guessed it—the sidewalk café at the new 'Paris end' of Collins Street.

1:E

MADAME BROOK & THE CORSET CASE

31 COLLINS STREET (ENTRANCE TO SOFITEL)

The toney department store of Buckley & Nunn used to stand alongside its rival Myer in Bourke Street. In 1900, Buckley's secured the services of an authentic Parisienne *couturière,* in the person of Madame Gabriella Brook, to keep its customers in step with the latest modes from Europe. Her Melbourne home was an apartment upstairs at Masonic Chambers, which stood right here.

For thirty years—first at Buckley's, then as head of costuming for the theatrical firm of J. C. Williamson—Madame Brook would be the first and last word in Melbourne chic. Here she was at the races in 1914:

> *Madame Brook wore a toilette which caused much comment, for the skirt seemed to be composed principally of purple beads, which opened to reveal purple hose and tiny buckskin shoes of the same colour. A coatee of Indian pink, which appeared to be only ninon, or at most marquisette, and a jaunty little purple tulle hat, were the complements.*

Ninon? Marquisette? And what was a coatee? No matter—she must have looked amazing. As an arbiter of fashion, she leaned into every caprice. One year she'd urge Melbourne women to show more leg—'Sydney women are far more daring in regard to the display of their limbs'—only to endorse, a year later, the revival of bustles and crinolines as 'a blessing for the woman who does not possess a Venus-like figure'.

Not long after she arrived in Melbourne, Madame Brook found herself embroiled in the cause célèbre of its day, the Corset Case. An American firm, Weingarten Bros. of New York, launched legal action in three Australian states to stop the sale of a British-made corset which it claimed copied its own product's patented 'bias goring'. Not only that: local retailers were accused of practising orchestrated deception. Enlisted as an industry spy by Weingarten's Melbourne agents, Madame Brook went to Treadway's department store and asked for a 'WB Erect Form' corset (the American brand), only to be fobbed off with a 'WB *correct* form', the cheaper British knock-off.

As expert witnesses in the case, Melbourne corsetiers were momentary celebrities, discoursing on 'the true inwardness of stays' and demonstrating the finer points of corset engineering. 'I suppose it gives more play to the figure,' mused the judge, examining the Erect Form's bias goring. In the Adelaide case Sir John Downer, for the defence, recoiled from a dove-grey corset and was taunted by the opposing counsel: 'I think Sir John should try this one on. But not in court.' (Sir John, incidentally, was the grandfather of Liberal Party veteran Alexander Downer who has often been depicted in cartoons wearing fishnet stockings and garters.)

It took twenty minutes on average to fit a buyer with a corset. Imagine making your living by wrangling women's juddery bits into submission. I had a corsetier for a grandmother, and she was just as stiff and unbending as you'd expect. My other grandmother wore an antique boned corset right up until she died, in 1971. It had laces longer than I was tall, and I liked to help her hook them zigzag up the back. It was the corset, in the end, that kept her upright.

A whole swathe of old Collins Street—all the way to the Exhibition Street corner—was pulled down in the early 1970s. Along with the Oriental Hotel and the Freemasons' Hall, there were low-rise buildings, like Masonic Chambers, housing the professional rooms of innumerable doctors and dentists.

Long before it was the Paris end, this was the *thermometer* end of Collins Street. Doctors set up shop here from the 1840s, when the elevated city-fringe location would have carried healthful associations. Of course, living 'above the shop', they made their homes here too. Dr Godfrey Howitt was one of the first—literally. His home and medical practice were at No. 1 Collins Street ('Howitt's Corner') set in a rambling garden that extended all the way to Flinders Lane. In fact, it was more like a farmlet, complete with orchard, vineyard and conservatories. Howitt Lane, at the rear, marks the edge of the doctor's garden, traces of which—overgrown camellias and a glorious spreading magnolia—survived right up to the 1950s.

Over time, doctors were joined at this end of Collins Street by dentists. Originally, doctors would have attended to their patients' dental needs. For those who couldn't afford a doctor's fee, there were barbers who dabbled in dentistry. There was even dentistry-as-entertainment, with extractions—the more theatrical, the better—performed in front of a crowd. From the 1870s onwards, dentists' use of nitrous oxide extended the fun to their patients. 'Laughing gas' was widely advertised by practitioners in Collins Street and elsewhere as a guarantee of *painless* dentistry. But there were frequent complaints of dentists assaulting sedated female patients, and you'd be amazed (or maybe not) at how easy it seems to have been for a fellow so charged simply to change his address and reoffend. There were stories, too, of patients released onto Collins Street, still 'tiddly' from the gas, posing a hazard to traffic, trams and themselves.

1:F

LOUISA BARROW'S HOUSE
CORNER SPRING & FLINDERS STREETS

Marjorie Theobald has written that, in the history of Victoria's goldfields, 'Women were nowhere, but women were everywhere.' The same is true of Melbourne in its first fifty years or more, only I'd change the emphasis and say instead that women were everywhere, but women were nowhere. Consider Louisa Barrow, who lived and raised her family in a house on this spot.

For thirty-four years from 1846 she was the all-but-wife of Sir Redmond Barry, prominent figure in Melbourne's evolution from Nowheresville to 'Queen City of the South'. They had a daughter and three sons together, but lived separately and their relationship—at least Sir Redmond's end of it—was an open one. (He kept a diary of his liaisons.) It was an open secret, too. When they met, Louisa Barrow was already married and their affair made for a scandal in small-town Melbourne. But it endured until Sir Redmond's death in 1880—and beyond: the two of them share a grave, though Louisa went unacknowledged on the headstone until 2016.

Sir Redmond Barry was in many ways an admirable Melburnian, and you'll meet him again in this book. When you do, remember Louisa.

This would have been the very edge of town when she set up house here in 1852. The Treasury Gardens were still bushland—though thinned out for firewood—and the road heading east, to the brickfields and Richmond, was wild enough to be the haunt of bushrangers by night. Charles La Trobe, governor of the new colony of Victoria—gloriously separated from New South Wales just the year before—would have passed this way to and from Jolimont, where he reigned as the Queen's representative in a pre-fab timber cottage (now relocated across the river to the Domain, near the Botanic Gardens).

Louisa's house was a step up from that. It would probably have been called a villa, one of several along this semi-rural stretch of Flinders Street at that time. Standing at the front door, you'd have looked out across, not train lines, but paddocks and swampland and the river bending away to the south.

The first of the rail lines heading eastward from the city was laid down in the 1870s. With Melbourne's galloping suburban growth of the 1880s, the sprawl of train tracks at this end of Flinders Street spread ever-wider, replacing the river view with an eyesore. In 1927 came the first proposal to 'beautify' the railyards by roofing them over and letting the city stretch towards the river, an idea that has resurfaced intermittently ever since. But now it seems there's a firm plan (at least, it *was* firm before COVID) to build a gazillion-storey tower over the railyards at Spring Street. We can be pretty sure that beautification isn't the point of the plan.

1:G

HERALD BUILDING

CORNER FLINDERS & EXHIBITION STREETS

We don't know if Louisa Barrow's house had a name, but the house that once stood on this corner did: Eltham, a three-storey mansion of eighteen bedrooms, surrounded by a vast walled garden. For a time in the 1890s it was occupied by the garrison mess, a military club during whose rowdy tenancy it was said that even the trees in the gardens 'stored up some strange stories'. By World War One the run-down mansion (renamed Normanhurst) was operating as a boarding house; still, it was the last city property to have a street-front garden.

The one-acre block was cleared in 1921 to make way for a five-storey temple to newsprint. Kicking off in 1840, when Melbourne was just five years old, the *Herald* would be the city's longest-running newspaper. It became an afternoon paper in 1869 and by the mid-twentieth century ran to seven editions a day, from the Home edition at midday to the Last Final Extra near dusk. Each fresh edition carried breaking news and the latest sports results, for eager consumption by the commuting hordes. At its peak in the mid-1960s, the *Herald* sold half a million copies a day, more than any other Australian newspaper.

This success was credited to Sir Keith Murdoch, father of Rupert. Between 1921 and his death in 1952, Sir Keith went from editor-in-chief to managing director to chairman, leading the newspaper and the company to ever greater heights and reach.

The *Herald*'s tabloid sibling was the *Sun News-Pictorial*, a morning paper first published in 1923, when this building was brand-new. The two papers merged in 1990, becoming the *Herald-Sun*. The last newspaper was printed here in 1995, when Rupert Murdoch's News Ltd moved its operations across the river.

I was a habitué of the Herald building for a time, when I was twenty or so. As part of my job I'd be sent to leaf through manila folders of glossy black-and-white photos in the picture library there. The Gotham-style building was designed to awe, and it did—all polished marble, lofty ceilings, wide corridors, smoky wood panelling. And you could sense, if not actually hear, the thunderous printing presses at work downstairs, urgently making the news.

1:H

JAMES SMITH'S COTTAGE
23 EXHIBITION STREET

From his front verandah, James Smith must have watched with pleasure as the Herald building took shape. In 1920 he'd moved from the house two doors down, in which he'd lived most of his fifty-eight years, into a tiny cottage built on this spot in 1844. His old home was replaced with a four-storey underclothing factory, built of reinforced concrete with a steel frame. But the veteran engineer wouldn't have felt a twinge. He'd been one of four experts who framed the Melbourne Building Act of 1916, green-lighting construction methods that would bring the city into the new century—and sweep away much of the old one.

Smith was all for modernity. He'd been on the panel that chose Walter Burley Griffin's as the winning design for Canberra. *And* he was the first to call for the roofing-over of the Jolimont railyards. The irony is that he lived in an antique.

As part of Melbourne's centenary celebrations, in 1935, a quest was mounted to identify the oldest surviving house (as opposed to, say, a church, public building or warehouse) in the CBD. Pinning down exact dates of origin proved tricky but, on the strength of 'a possibility—even a strong probability', James Smith's brick-and-stone cottage at

23 Collins Place* won the gong. Aside from its age, it would have been among the few houses left standing in central Melbourne. But not for long. After Smith's death in 1940 it lasted just a year.

For better or worse, heritage wasn't a thing back then. People expressed occasional misgivings that 'Old Melbourne is disappearing', but progress trumped sentimentality every time.

1:1

AC/DC LANE

Buildings and landmarks may rise and fall, but at least we have the city's streets as steady bearings. Or do we?

For more than a hundred years, this lane had a perfectly serviceable name: Corporation Lane. I read somewhere that all Melbourne's unnamed rights of way were officially known as corporation lanes—i.e. belonging to the city corporation, or council. But not all were signposted. This one was, because it gave access to the corporation yard. Here, in an age before hi-vis vests and leaf blowers, were kept the road-rollers, the mowing machines, the Men at Work signs, the wheelbarrows and pushcarts and shovels for leaning on. Earlier still, it led to a bottle-oh's yard.

* From 1880 until 1963, the stretch of Exhibition Street between Flinders and Collins went by the name Collins Place.

In 2004 it was someone's (or some committee's) groovy idea to rebrand Corporation Lane as AC/DC Lane. Never mind that Acka Dacka were Sydney lads: hadn't they cruised along Swanston Street on a flatbed truck in their 1975 video for 'It's a Long Way to the Top (If You Wanna Rock 'n' Roll)'? (See 5:D.) Justification enough to erase the prosaic Corporation Lane.

The slash (/) or lightning bolt between AC and DC wasn't included on the street sign as it contravened rules set by the Registrar of Geographic Names. In a suitably hellraising gesture, a huge lightning bolt was added by a local artist. And it wasn't the first time this laneway had witnessed a remarkable bolt. One Friday in 1907, a delivery cart pulled by two horses was parked in Corporation Lane when a gas engine backfired at a nearby factory and the horses bolted. Off they went, full-tilt down Flinders Lane, the cart colliding with several others before it was halted by the iron post of a hotel verandah in Swanston Street. 'Sensational Bolt' ran the headline in the *Herald*'s next edition.

Launching AC/DC Lane in 2004, Lord Mayor John So ended with an invocation to 'Let us rock.' Well, if pop-culture cool is the game, why not go the whole hog and rebrand the city Batmania?* (Maybe because of the corporate clash with Marvel Stadium.)

---

* Batmania, in honour of founding citizen John Batman, was among the names originally proposed for the town that would become Melbourne.

Names attach to places, places attach to names, and memories attach to both. *Vale*, Corporation Lane.

1:J

HATPIN END

RUSSELL STREET, SOUTH END

This stretch of Russell Street, between Flinders and Collins, used to be the Hatpin End. In the decades before and after women won the vote (1901 federally, 1908 for state elections), women's organisations clustered here. On one Flinders Lane corner was the Women's Christian Temperance Union (WCTU), a leading force in the suffrage movement; on the other was the Victorian Vigilance Association, which in the 1890s campaigned to end sexual victimisation of women and girls (a movement that led to the age of consent being raised from twelve to sixteen). There were also the Young Women's Christian Union coffee rooms, the Girls' Friendly Society Lodge, a couple of female-run servants' registries and an agency for trained nurses.

Not far from here, in Flinders Street, a nurse named Mae Hussey would be the first person charged with wearing an 'unprotected' hatpin, under a city by-law introduced in 1913. A fashion for extravagantly large hats—crinolines for the head—necessitated hatpins so long that they posed a public-health risk. The hats' elevation meant that it was men who were most in danger of being skewered by the protruding point of a 'murderous' hatpin. To meet the emergency, hatpin protectors—tiny metal knobs that clipped on the points—were sold for sixpence each. The by-law required women not only to fit their hatpins with protectors (even a bottle cork would do), but to carry spares at all times. Mae Hussey's claim that her protector must have fallen off cut no ice with the council inspector, who fined her ten shillings.

The WCTU stayed on here in Russell Street long past its heyday. By the time six o'clock closing (one of its signal achievements) came to an end in 1966, the organisation would be sharing premises with the Elly Lukas model agency.

I wonder if the confluence of 'women's business' at this end of Russell Street owed something to the presence of the Society of Friends' meeting house, near the Flinders Street corner. Melbourne's Quakers met there for almost a hundred years, until 1953, promoting pacifism and fellowship across cultures. The old Friends meeting house would be replaced by the headquarters of the Girl Guides, a spin-off of a quasi-militaristic movement grounded in imperialism. But the Quaker spirit hadn't entirely left the building: as a Brownie, I earned my basket-weaving badge there.

NEWSPAPER BLOCKADE
HOSIER LANE

In 1895 the *Herald* introduced linotype machinery, throwing many of its compositors out of work in the midst of a worldwide economic depression. Before linotype, a newspaper compositor had to lay out every line of type letter by letter and back-to-front—and at speed. With linotype, the operator used a keyboard to compose lines of type ready for casting into metal printing plates.

The laid-off *Herald* compositors began a rival afternoon newspaper, the *Evening News*, with offices and printing works in Hosier Lane. But on the day the first edition was due to appear, the Board of Works unexpectedly dug up the road at both ends of the laneway, cutting off the *Evening News* 'from all vehicular communication with the outside world'. The *News* was going nowhere.

The *Herald*'s own works, at that time, were right next door in Flinders Street, making the blockage of Hosier Lane look a lot like proto-Murdochian bastardry. The *Evening News* would fold after just six months.

1:L

SEVERED HAND
210 FLINDERS LANE
(ENTRY TO WESTIN HOTEL UNDERGROUND CAR PARK)

On this spot one afternoon in October 1880, passers-by encountered 'a most ghastly spectacle'. Lying on the ledge of a shop window was a human hand in an advanced state of decomposition. Some boys had found it in the middle of the street and kicked it around for a while before they lost interest.

'Whatever tale of foul murder it may have to tell,' said the *Herald*, 'cannot yet be ascertained.' But some wondered whether the hand might belong to 'the long-missing Mrs Farrell'.

Who was this Mrs Farrell? Two years earlier, twenty-eight-year-old Elizabeth Farrell had been reported missing from her Collingwood home. Her relatives cast suspicion on Elizabeth's violent husband and his brother, but police dismissed it as a domestic matter. Only after the newspapers took an interest in 'the Farrell mystery' was a pair of detectives sent in. They pulled up the Farrells' floorboards, dug up the backyard, dredged the river and searched the Collingwood manure depot. Nothing. Four years would pass: Mr Farrell and his brother both died, Elizabeth's children were sent to an orphanage and the tumbledown house in Montague Street was sold for demolition. The wreckers' work was nearly done when, under the hearthstone, they found a mass of bones—only to let a rag-and-bone man take them away before police were notified. Some of the bones would be retrieved, but too few for an inquest.

The severed hand found in Flinders Lane was sent to Dr Youl the coroner for investigation. Many had speculated that it was an amputation, thrown into the river then washed up by recent floods. (An amputated arm had been fished out of the Yarra not long before.) But no, the hand—of a woman or small man, with tapering fingers—was found to have rotted off and had evidently been preserved in spirits as a specimen. How it ended up in Flinders Lane was anyone's guess.

This stretch of Flinders Lane, through to Elizabeth Street, was traditionally associated with the rag trade. Not literal rags, but *schmattes*, the garment industry. Back when 'Made in Melbourne' was a commonplace, the lane burst at its seams with workrooms and factories, textile agents and importers. They employed between them thousands of women and girls (including my mum) as designers, cutters and machinists. Even now, with Etsy the storefront for locally made fashion, you can still find small-scale ateliers tucked away in and around Flinders Lane.

For forty years or more, Maria George Ltd, importers of 'sequins, beads, dress stones, etc.', was just uphill from here. When I was maybe sixteen and passing this way en route to the inevitable bus stop, I bumped into Pam, a girl who ranked, in our daggy off-the-rack suburb, as a fashion maven. On the bus ride home she showed me the pearly seeds and teardrops she'd bought to illuminate some creation of hers. That's how I came to associate Maria George with a twinkly kind of glamour way out of my league. Now I hear it's relocated across Swanston Street to the Nicholas Building—if not the heart, at least a major organ of Melbourne's artisanal rag trade.

1:M

CATHEDRAL HOTEL

CORNER FLINDERS LANE & SWANSTON STREET

Albert Williams arrived by ship from England on 15 December 1891. During his twenty-eight days in Melbourne, he would change his name four times and kill his wife.

Like Elizabeth Farrell, Emily Williams was buried under the hearth of a cottage fireplace. The cottage was in Windsor, newly leased to a man who called himself Druin. A week after Emily's death, her husband took a room at the hotel that stood on this spot, the Cathedral, under the surname Duncan. On hotel stationery he wrote to Holt's Matrimonial Agency seeking an introduction to a young woman with a view to marriage: 'She must be good looking, age eighteen or twenty, and know something of housekeeping.' Duncan failed to keep an appointment at Holt's. Instead, as Harry Dawson, he sold his murdered wife's effects and paid for some jewellery with a forged cheque, before taking the name Baron Swanston (after Swanston Street, presumably) and boarding a ship for Sydney. On the voyage, he met Kate Rounsefell and within days they were engaged.

Emily had been dead just three weeks. Her body would be discovered in early March, triggering a manhunt for the Windsor murderer. By then, Baron Swanston was on the West Australian goldfields and his fiancée was sailing from Sydney to join him. When Kate's ship put in at Melbourne, she was met by a telegram from her sister: 'For God's sake, go no further.'

Albert Williams' real name, it turned out, was Frederick Deeming. Arrested in Western Australia, he was being escorted back to Melbourne when police searching his former home in Lancashire uncovered the bodies of Deeming's first wife and their four children. There followed calls for his extradition to England, where he'd have had to answer for five murders instead of one. But he could only be hanged once—and he was, at Melbourne Gaol on 23 May 1892.

Today, Deeming reads as a straight-up psychopath. Some in the press speculated that he may have been Jack the Ripper (the dates and his whereabouts roughly lined up) and he half-hinted they were right. He's still among the suspects.

1:N

LADIES ONLY SEATS
SWANSTON STREET

'Combining chivalry with utilitarianism', the city council in 1934 ruled that some of the seats beside St Paul's Cathedral would be 'set apart for womenfolk'. These seats opposite the busy Flinders Street station were a popular spot for people-watching. They were even said to be a substitute for 'the non-existent city square'. The problem was that 'men usurped more than a fair share of the accommodation'.

So the words Ladies Only were marked out in white tiles at the entrance to one of the seating alcoves. But as a newspaper commentator would remark, 'The tilers might have saved themselves the trouble':

> *The summer brought the familiar sight of elderly women laden with parcels gazing wistfully at the seats, occupied by men.*

Perhaps the sign was too subtle? The edict was amplified, in painted letters sixty centimetres tall—which seemed to have some effect, only 'it wore off with the paint'. From time to time council workers would touch up the lettering, always under the watchful eye of men seated there.

In my teens I used to congregate with male friends on the Ladies Only seats, thinking we were sticking it to 'the man'. How wrong can you be? What was needed, of course, was a hatpin.

WALK 2

COMPLETE WITH ASPIDISTRA

In which we stick close to the Yarra without ever seeing it and climb a hill that's not there

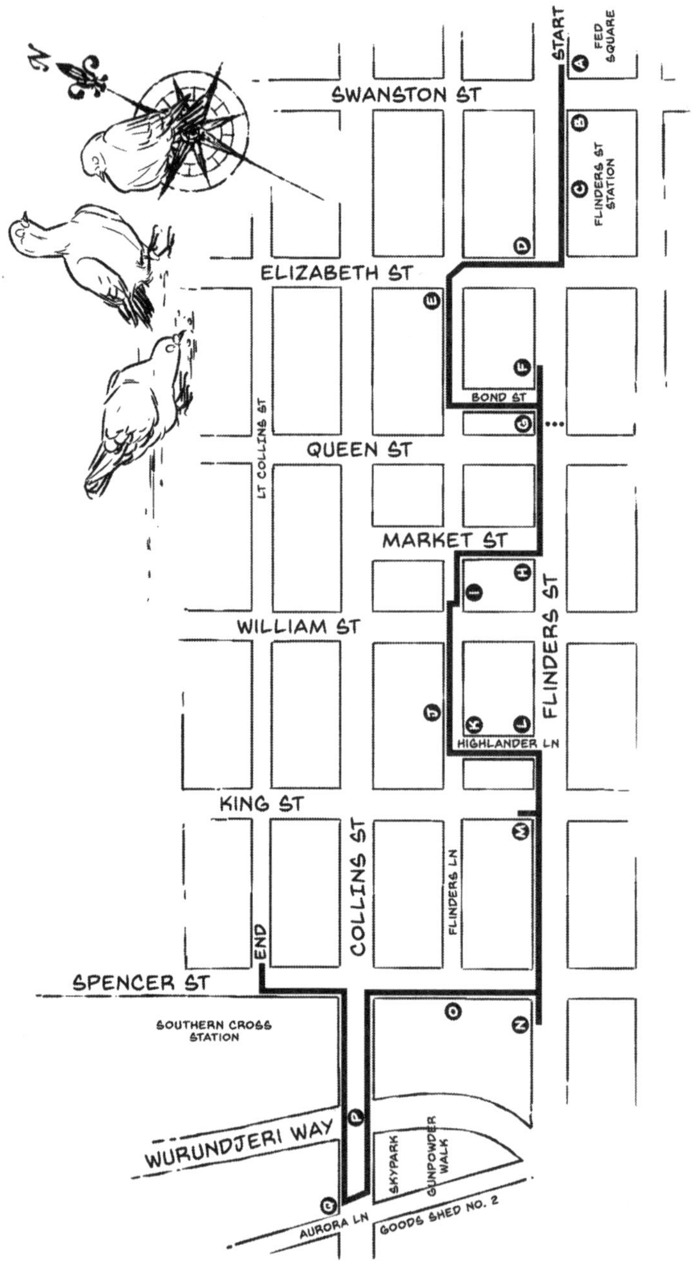
START
FED SQUARE
FLINDERS ST STATION
SWANSTON ST
ELIZABETH ST
BOND ST
QUEEN ST
LT COLLINS ST
MARKET ST
WILLIAM ST
FLINDERS ST
HIGHLANDER LN
KING ST
COLLINS ST
FLINDERS LN
END
SPENCER ST
SOUTHERN CROSS STATION
WURUNDJERI WAY
SKYPARK
GUNPOWDER WALK
AURORA LN
GOODS SHED NO. 2

2:A

MORGUE
FEDERATION SQUARE

On this corner Melbourne's morgue once stood. The ostentatious location seems to suggest there was a literal acceptance, in the nineteenth century, of the proposition that 'in the midst of life we are in death'. And indeed, a birth or marriage could be registered at the office next door.

The morgue was on this spot for perhaps twenty-five years, after which its location would wander. But it never wandered far from the river—for convenience, I guess, as hardly a day passed without a body being fished out. Whether from drunken misadventure, suicide, murder or plain bad luck, it was no rare thing for a Melburnian to end up dead in the sluggish Yarra.

Women and newborns accounted for many of the river dead. Because...what could you do if you were poor, single and pregnant? The options for any single woman boiled down to 'marry, stitch, die or do worse'. Yes, Victorian social values ranked prostitution as 'worse' than death. And so to the river.

That severed hand found in Flinders Lane in 1880 would have been brought here for the coroner's opinion. Not long after, the morgue made way for Princes Bridge station, terminus of the railways that converged on Melbourne from the east. Still overseen by the veteran Dr Youl, the morgue relocated across the railyards, nearer to the river's edge.

2:B

FLINDERS STREET STATION

The mouth of the station entrance—Luna Park with clocks in place of teeth—was the pre-eminent image of twentieth-century Melbourne. The tidal flow of pedestrians through the station mouth was the stuff of nature documentaries. During the filming of the 1959 movie *On the Beach,* actors Ava Gardner and Gregory Peck came close to being trampled when they staged a clinch on Swanston Street amid post-theatre crowds headed for the station.

By the 1930s, Flinders Street station was the busiest in the world, swallowing and disgorging more than twice as many passengers weekly as Grand Central station in New York. Nippy paperboys and chain-smoking news vendors would sell close to ten thousand copies of the *Herald* there each afternoon. (Back then Melbourne commuters were adept at the now-lost art of manipulating broadsheet pages in a confined space.)

The Elizabeth Street end of the station site had been dedicated to railway business since 1854, as city terminus of the Port Melbourne train line, the colony's first. But before the present station was erected, the Swanston Street frontage was occupied by Melbourne's riverside fish market. When the fishmongers relocated in the early 1890s, the site languished for more than a decade, hosting a ramshackle assortment of stalls—and a 'bicycle stable'.

Melbourne lost its mojo, along with its standing as Australia's leading city, during the crash and slump of the 1890s. Flinders Street station was the city's big gesture of renewal. The huge pile, four years in the making, opened in 1909. From the start, taste-makers dismissed the station's architecture as florid and vulgar. But that missed the point: Flinders Street station was a palace for the people. It was designed to be not just a place to catch a train, but the civic and social heart of the working city. Upstairs, above the station concourse, were a massive ballroom, a crêche and a maze of rooms where the Victorian Railway Institute held its clubs and classes including fencing, table tennis, wrestling, photography, calisthenics and ham radio. And, of course, 'under the clocks' became the great Melbourne rendezvous.

In the philistine 1960s, a plan was hatched to raze Flinders Street station and build in its place a sixty-storey tower, with the station relegated to a subterranean plaza. To be called Flinders Gate (shades of *Heaven's Gate*), the project would be championed by successive state governments and city councils. Only when the station was on the brink of demolition was Flinders Gate scuttled. 'In dubious expiation' (as Alan Bennett would say) the sooty station building was treated to a good scrubbing and a fresh coat of paint.

It'll be interesting to see where the new Metro Tunnel leaves Flinders Street station. Commuter traffic through Flinders Street dropped when the City Loop, with three stations in the CBD, opened in 1980. With two more stations along Swanston Street, Flinders Street station is at risk of becoming a has-been. What then? The grand ballroom has been a pigeon roost for years now. I'll bet someone's eyeing it for apartments.

2:C

THE LOUNGERS' CLUB

FLINDERS STREET, OPPOSITE DEGRAVES STREET

There was nowhere under the clocks of the new Flinders Street station to sit or shelter from the weather. The seats beside St Paul's Cathedral, in view of the clocks, were invariably monopolised by manspreaders. Luckily for the foot-weary female traveller there was the Loungers' Club.

Under the management of Ada Gunn, the Loungers'

Club opened, behind this grilled window, in the basement of the new station in 1909. Melbourne had numerous clubs for men—the Yorick, the Athenaeum and of course the Melbourne Club—but, before the Loungers' Club, none for women. For a penny (or an annual fee of one guinea), a woman could freshen up, write and post a letter, make a phone call or just lounge on a sofa while waiting for 'unpunctual friends'. Tea and scones cost threepence and the newspapers could be read for free. The club was fitted up like a middle-class parlour, complete with aspidistra, tasteful pictures on the walls, bookshelves and a wickerwork whatnot, all keyed in a colour scheme of bronze, green and pale mauve.

The civic-minded spirit of the Loungers' Club was in keeping with the new station. Evidently it was seen as not just an amenity but a proud innovation. 'Melbourne people are very much inclined,' said one of the papers, 'to think that America, or even Sydney, must always have superior comforts, facilities, and conveniences in every way.' (I like that *or even Sydney*.) But did Toledo or Sydney have a Loungers' Club, where an office girl could sit and eat her sandwiches out of the weather, or change her blouse, put her face on and do her hair before a night out in town?

Open till 11.30 at night, the Loungers' Club hosted regular meetings of terrier- and poultry-fanciers and the Unlicensed Chemists' Assistants Association. Ahead of the 1910 federal election, candidates canvassed women voters there, prompting this broadside in the press—

> *Women again. What is not politics doing for the women? God help Australia when women begin to take the place of men in clubs hitherto sacred to male loungers.*

The Loungers' Club caved soon after, opening a smoke lounge for men and selling cigars at the refreshments window. A Mrs Walker ('well known in ice skating and croquet circles') took over from Ada Gunn in 1915 and would eventually move the Loungers' Club to the other side of Flinders Street, after which this basement area became the station cafeteria.

2:D

FLOODS, WATERWORKS

CORNER FLINDERS & ELIZABETH STREETS

Not much more than a year after Flinders Street station opened, a heavy summer downpour flooded the Elizabeth Street subway and station basement almost to knee-depth. (Loungers' Club, ahoy!) But: 'There is no likelihood of the subways being flooded in the future,' the railway commissioners assured the *Herald*. Bold words.

In fact, Elizabeth Street, the street that divides the two ends of town, would (and will) always flood, because it marks the crease between Melbourne's hills. It's a gully, a creek-in-waiting, a tributary of the Yarra, the natural course of the city's stormwater. As Toni Morrison wrote: 'All water has a perfect memory...'

In Melbourne's early decades, the Elizabeth Street gully was in its near-natural state, with no underground drainage, no gutters, no footpaths to speak of. But it was also a busy thoroughfare lined with shops. To traverse it in wet weather called for sturdy boots and temerity. Semi-permanent water features included Lake Cashmore and the River Enscoe, treacherous spots near the Collins Street corner, both named for long-suffering storekeepers in that vicinity. People even spoke of the 'post office coast', up near Bourke Street, where legend tells of an entire bullock team swallowed up in a mud-hole. (See 5:J)

At least once in every decade the old waterway reasserts itself and, when it does, no amount of plumbing can contain it. Flinders Street station, thwarting its route to the river, invariably gets the knee-deep treatment. Surely the station's Elizabeth Street subway was *meant* to double as a drain, no matter what the railway commissioners may have said.

It makes sense that—before there was a station, before there were railways—there should have been a water-works at this corner. For a few years from 1849, water was pumped from the dirty Yarra to a filtration tank here and sold for household use at the rate of a penny a barrel. With the advent of trains, a tank atop a timber tower (perhaps it was the same one?) at the original Elizabeth Street station entrance supplied water for the locomotive steam engines.

When, in 1883, the station took on a more substantial shape, a new tower replaced the old one on this spot. Instead of a water tank, it supported Melbourne's first landmark clock, known ever after as the Water Tower Clock. Its watery connection was finally broken in 1905, when work began on the new station and the clock tower relocated to Spencer Street station, where it would be a fixture for another sixty years. The four-faced clock that still perches high above the Elizabeth Street station entrance became the keeper of railway time in Melbourne, visible from all points of the commuters' compass.

2:E

AUSTRALIAN BUILDING

CORNER ELIZABETH STREET & FLINDERS LANE

The Australian Building, on this spot, was for sixty years the tallest in Melbourne.

A visitor to the city in 1883 noted, 'The climate and the comparative cheapness of land give the colonists an aversion to height in their buildings.' That may have been so. Mainly, though, tall buildings were unpopular while they relied on stairs to reach the upper floors.

Elevators enabled the Australian Building—and its

tenants—to reach twelve storeys in height. Those early lifts were run by hydraulic power. High-pressure water was pumped underground throughout the city from a plant in present-day Docklands. (In some laneways there are still metal cover-plates stamped Hydraulic Power Dpt, marking old service ports.) Rather than being raised by cables, the lifts in the Australian Building were pushed upwards by an iron plunger which, as the force of water from below was reduced, would gradually descend. Touted as the safest of elevator technologies, it meant that a shaft for the plunger had to be sunk as deep *below* the building as the lifts went high. That was a challenge in this, the lowest-lying part of the city. The miners who were brought in to dig the lift shaft through wet, unstable ground had megafauna bones and ancient tree trunks to contend with.

In its day—it was finished in 1890—the Australian Building rivalled contemporary skyscrapers in New York and Chicago and, for more than twenty years, would be taller (*even!*) than anything in Sydney. How typical of Melbourne, though, to choose the city's lowest elevation as the site for its tallest building.

The depression of the 1890s ended Melbourne's boom years and, soon after, a height limit of forty metres was imposed on new city builds. At forty-five metres, the Australian Building was *too* tall: no fire hose could reach its upper storeys, and for a building with timber floors that posed a real danger. Besides (the thinking went), if skyscrapers were allowed to proliferate, even Melbourne's broad streets might become gloomy canyons. The city's height limit would hold firm until ICI House broke it in 1958. (See 4:A.) The Australian Building, stripped of glory, would be demolished in 1980.

It was a fairly undistinguished structure, especially as it grew sooty with age and was overshadowed by the city's upward progress. (In its dying days, even heritage advocates couldn't find much to say in its favour, beyond that it demonstrated 'a strong texture, mainly through the multitude of windows and a relationship of solids to voids'.) But it's rather remarkable to think of a skyscraper built entirely of brick, with dormer windows and a slate-roofed turret. In old photos, what most stands out is the soaring slab of the windowless north wall, which for decades bore a gigantic endorsement for Sunlight soap (*Good for the clothes. Good for the hands that wash the clothes*), legible the full length of Elizabeth Street. There would have been river views from all but the lowest storeys, and skylights in the roof made the top floor prized as a photographic studio. Like all city buildings of the period, the Australian Building operated on the (unintentionally) socialistic principle that the best view was reserved for its live-in caretaker, whose lodgings were 'on the roof'.

On the afternoon of the Australian Building's official opening, the entire board of the company that owned it crowded into one of the lifts, bound for the top floor. The

dozen men included Alfred Deakin and other notables who, had they but known it, would lose everything in the coming financial crash. The lift driver tugged a rope…too vigorously perhaps, because the lift shot up like a rocket. Luckily, safety springs at the top of the shaft cushioned the lift's impact (it recoiled a mere three metres) so that, in *this* crash, the only casualties were hats. Waiting to greet the shaken dignitaries was the building's architect, Henry Kemp, who would later write:

> *What a sensation in the city of that day if suddenly had emerged from its highest building a rocket with a dripping tail 100 feet long, topped by a crushed lift cage, from which dropped at intervals into the Yarra or on the railway buildings some of its best known citizens!*

They all, Kemp noted, chose the stairs for their descent.

Something along the lines of Kemp's gleeful fantasy actually came to pass in 1893—only the result was far from comic. William Ellis, a house painter, had collected his week's wages in Flinders Lane and was nearing the corner of Elizabeth Street, opposite here, holding his little daughter Daisy by the hand. From out of the sky came a lump of jagged iron, maybe three kilograms in weight. It missed Daisy but not her father, who was killed. A winding-engine had exploded on a building site two hundred metres away, showering the city centre with metal shards and fragments of the unfortunate engine-driver. Flinders Lane could be treacherous.

CITY BASEMENT BOOKS

342 FLINDERS STREET (VIA FLINDERS LANE)

Flinders Lane, if you can believe it, was originally Melbourne's premier street. At the first land sale, in 1837, allotments in the lane fetched higher prices than those in Collins Street. Its appeal was that it was close to the river—entry point to the town—but not close enough for inundation. Flinders Street then was riverfront and, for much of its length, dedicated to the docks. It was Flinders *Lane* that would be the first street of commerce—the first dry land—a newcomer arrived at.

In the 1850s a Yankee merchant compared Flinders Lane with New York's Wall Street. Things had changed by the turn of the century, when it was so choked with factories and warehouses that a dray barely fitted between the gutters, and a partisan Melburnian journalist could disparage Sydney's principal thoroughfares by likening them to Flinders Lane.

Now plunge down Bond Street to Flinders Street, turn left, and keep your eye out for an open doorway under the sign City Basement Books, with steep stairs leading down. Take those stairs (holding on to the handrail).

Everything about this branching cavern of a shop enchants me. The books, of course. Books! What's the oldest and cheapest you can find here? Ancient books, covers loose or missing but rag-paper pages full of interest, can be had for as little as a dollar or two. On my first visit after the COVID lockdown in 2020, I discovered a room I'd never noticed before (how was that possible?) where the oldest and raggedest books are kept. Under a stack of old volumes of *Encyclopedia Britannica* was a family bible hand-dated 1824. And I picked up an epistolary novel published in 1775, with its covers rattled loose but the marbled endpapers still vivid yolk-yellow and scarlet. Two prior owners had left inscriptions, one summarising the plot in sepia ink on the title page. Reader, I bought it—for three dollars.

Apart from the books, though, what made me bring you down here is the very fact of its *down*ness. Any opportunity to get literally under the city's skin is worth a look. Not that there's anything specially subterranean to *see* here; but it lets us consider the city underground.

Like every city worth its salt, Melbourne has rumoured secret passageways and sealed-up tunnels snaking beneath its streets. (See 3:Q, 4:C.) Here, near the waterfront, were bond stores with thick-walled cellars for storing imported perishables and booze. Below the foundations of long-standing city buildings, archaeologists have found remnants of walls with windows, which must once have stood *above* ground level. I know a couple who, as students in the 1940s, worked at the Ball & Welch department store in Flinders Street (opposite Fed Square) and remember just such a fragment of wall—bluestone, with a bricked-up window—posing a puzzle in the basement staffroom there. Even in a city as un-ancient as Melbourne, ground and street levels have changed over time, built up against flooding or to smooth out bumps, or dug away to reduce a steep slope. In places, the old surface has been buried; in others, the level we walk on was once way underground.

If the book-covered walls of City Basement Books reveal nothing about the past lives or former elevation of this spot, they point to something else: books are heavy, and basements—with solid ground beneath—are made for load-bearing. This isn't (quite) the last of Melbourne's basement bookshops. But, trust me, it's the best.*

2:G

ICEHOUSE, THE FALLS

FLINDERS STREET, OPPOSITE QUEEN STREET CORNER

In the summer of 1855 an icehouse was built on the dock-side at the foot of Queen Street, opposite. On its way from Boston, USA, was a shipload (more than five hundred tonnes) of river ice, some of it from the neighbourhood of Thoreau's Walden Pond. It was packed in sawdust

* I think of it as a direct descendant of Dwight's book shop (see 3:T).

for shipping and, once landed, was sold in blocks to fishmongers and hotels serving ice-cold drinks. Sandwiched between coal depots, the icehouse—double-brick walled and insulated with wood shavings—would stand here for ten years, receiving and storing imported ice until there was a reliable supply of the locally made article to be had.

Behind the icehouse, directly in line with Queen Street, a ragged ledge of rocks broke the surface of the Yarra. This was the Falls, the obstacle that originally determined the site of Melbourne. Ships approaching from the bay couldn't pass this point. They would anchor and turn in 'the Pond', a bulge in the river just below the Falls.

Upstream from here, the Yarra water changed from brackish to fresh. Along the river's edge between the Falls and Princes Bridge, bathing enclosures (called floating baths) operated in the early days. They would move progressively upriver as the Yarra became fouled by noxious industries.

Before there was a bridge at Swanston Street, a punt carried people and loads across the river above the Falls. At low tide, plucky Melburnians used the rocky ledge itself as a place to cross or fish from, just as the Woiwurrung people had long done. John Batman, landing here in 1835 after transacting the 'purchase' of land from the Woiwurrung, thought *Yarra Yarra* was the name of the river. In fact it meant 'fast-flowing', and referred to the rapids at the Falls. (The river itself was *Birrarung*.) Ten years later, Batman's son and namesake, fishing for schnapper from the rocks there, would lose his footing and drown in the Yarra.

The basalt boulders of the Falls formed a kind of natural dam wall which, in the event of heavy rain, slowed the flow from upstream, causing the river to break its banks and inundate ground floors and basements of warehouses all along Flinders Street. Dry goods—flour, sugar, salt—stored in sacks were the main casualties; something like three thousand tonnes of salt were lost in a flood at Christmas-time 1863. Eventually, as a mitigation measure, in 1883 the Falls were blasted away with dynamite.

2:H

CUSTOMS HOUSE

CORNER FLINDERS & MARKET STREETS

All this talk of the river, and we haven't even clapped eyes on it. Sure, if you really *want* to see Melbourne's brown river, by all means make a detour across Flinders Street and under the hulking railway viaduct. But *not* seeing the Yarra is more to the point.

Historically, Melbourne turned its back on the river to which it owed its existence. City-side, the Yarra was a working river, not a beauty spot. On this side were the docks; opposite were meatworks, tanneries, brickyards and factories, spewing effluent into the river. The ultimate ignominy, though, was the railway viaduct, built around

1890 to link Flinders and Spencer Street stations and, in the process, cutting the river off from the city. It would take another hundred years for the Yarra to be rediscovered and glamorised, once the factories on the other side were cleared away and specious Southbank raised in their place.

Standing here now and facing riverwards, there's nothing to see but a snaggle of road and rail. But here was Melbourne's starting-point. As his boat idled on the Pond in June 1835, John Batman wrote with certitude: 'This will be the place for a village.' And it very soon was.

Practically from the start, Melbourne was a planned and policed settlement. Batman's land 'purchase' was ruled invalid by the Sydney government, who instead claimed this territory for the King. Within two years of Batman's epiphany on the Pond, the 'village' had been named in honour of the British prime minister, Lord Melbourne. Homegrown toponyms like Batmania or Bearbrass—let alone Birrarung—never stood a chance.

To impose order on the place, officials were sent from Sydney, along with soldiers and convict labourers. Surveyors set to work, replacing the unruly shape of the initial settlement with a town laid out in a grid. Streets were named (after royalty, explorers, government officials and their wives) and allotments sold by auction—all except those set aside for government purposes, like the Customs reserve.

The siting here of the Customs House (now the

Immigration Museum) confirms the centrality of this spot to the original conception of Melbourne. Facing Flinders Street, it was the welcoming committee, the implacable face of officialdom, dockside. The tea examiner had his office here and so did the jerquer, whose job it was to inspect vessels for concealed goods. It occasionally happened in the early days that a runaway female convict would be smuggled across from Van Diemen's Land (Tasmania) in a beer barrel with the bung-hole left open. Just picture it: a 'contraband lady', cramped and crumpled, uncasked by a jerquer with a clipboard.

2:1

FAWKNER'S HOTEL

FLINDERS LANE, BETWEEN MARKET & WILLIAM STREETS

Look at a map of Melbourne's regimented street grid, and Market Street stands out as an interloper, an irregularity. As wide as the city's 'great' streets, it runs only as far as Collins Street. This stub marks a link with the pre-grid settlement. From the landing-place, it led straight to the original heart of the town.

The pre-survey settlement was clustered in this vicinity, a safe distance from the river and roughly in line with the future Flinders Lane. The germ of the neighbourhood—of the whole settlement—was a rough timber structure set back from what's now the corner of Flinders Lane and William Street. It was the house of John Pascoe Fawkner. Having sealed the deal with the Woiwurrung, John Batman headed back to Van Diemen's Land to celebrate. But when he returned to take possession of his 'purchase', the upstart Johnny Fawkner (and a handful of others) had beaten him to it. Though a teetotaller himself, Fawkner had brought over from Launceston not just building materials but a supply of beer, wine and spirits. No sooner was its shingle roof raised than his house became Fawkner's Hotel, with a bar in the front room (facing the river) and drinks liberally diluted with Yarra water.

When the town grid was laid out, Fawkner's Hotel was found to occupy part of the Customs reserve and he was paid to relinquish it. The facing block, sloping uphill towards Collins Street, was also reserved for government purposes and, early on, housed the police office-cum-courthouse and lock-up. Here also were the stocks, where minor transgressors would be secured by the legs (or by one leg, if female) to feel the sting of public opprobrium. Overhead, from the carcass of a river red gum, a bell hung as a fire siren.

From 1841, the reserve was dedicated to a public market and an arcade of stalls was put up. Rabbits imported from Van Diemen's Land, escaping from their seller, burrowed under the building and began to multiply. The stocks stayed put in the market square, which seems right. But the centre of town had already shifted, and the market here would never really flourish. When another market was established at the more popular east end of town, this one was designated the Western Market. In the early 1850s, as Melbourne struggled to absorb the incoming flood of gold-seekers, the Western Market became a makeshift campground and staging-post for new arrivals. On the Flinders Lane side, immigrants who had too much baggage for the long haul to the goldfields would line the roadway with their open trunks and kitbags, selling off the excess in an improvised street-market known as Rag Fair.

2:J

RIALTO HIGH-RISE TOILETS

472 FLINDERS LANE

Look up. Projecting from a brick wall beside the Intercontinental Hotel entrance is a corrugated-iron enclosure stretching five storeys high. It seems an incongruous feature for the ornate Rialto, built fronting Collins Street in 1890 by one of Melbourne's more flamboyant boom-time property developers. This was the Rialto's aerial outhouse—a five-storey urinal—thrust as far away as possible from the business end of things.

In the 1980s, a campaign to preserve the urinals saved this rear portion of the old Rialto building from demolition. Their workaday fabric and function were emblematic of a kind of utilitarian structure just then beginning to be dignified as 'heritage'. Not that they're entirely utilitarian. Painted brick-red as camouflage, and with wrought-iron railings and Gothic windows echoing those of the Rialto proper, they're (literally) several steps up from your average privy.

2:K

CASASSA & RAVENNA'S PASTA WORKS

485 FLINDERS LANE (CORNER HIGHLANDER LANE)

At this corner stood Messrs Casassa and Ravenna's Italian Manufactory, making macaroni and vermicelli. The pair arrived from San Francisco in 1862 and, to begin with, their factory relied on grain imported from California too, as the requisite 'strong' wheat wasn't yet grown locally. A horse-powered mill first ground the wheat to semolina then mixed it to a paste, which was extruded, cut and laid out to dry for several days. The factory could turn out five *tonnes* of pasta a week—that's a lot of macaroni—and sold it for just a trifle more than the imported article.

I dare say that, except for the horse, Casassa and Ravenna's process is much the same as that by which pasta is still made. But that it happened *here* is a reminder that there was a time—up until fifty or sixty years ago—when the central city was full of people *making things*. To leaf through a city directory of Casassa and Ravenna's era is to encounter a host of artisans and manufactories, each with their specialty: makers of ship's biscuits, ginger beer, cabbage-tree hats, brass instruments, buttons and dies, saddles and horse collars, coaches and wagons, lead pipe, agricultural tools, ovens, guns, paper bags, bagatelle tables, tents and flags, barrels, baskets, cutlery, watches, artificial flowers and bent-glass cases for jewellers' shops. All made here, in the streets and lanes of central Melbourne.

2:L

ROYAL HIGHLANDER HOTEL

CORNER FLINDERS STREET & HIGHLANDER LANE

After seventy-odd years on this spot, the Royal Highlander Hotel closed down at the end of 1910. It was one of many hotels condemned as surplus to the city's requirements. You've heard the expression 'a pub on every corner'? In Melbourne, by the end of the nineteenth century, that was literally true—and not just the corners of the main streets, but of almost every laneway. Such a boozed-up culture contributed to crime, poverty and premature death, as well as violence and misery for countless women and children. The influence of the temperance movement (and female voters) finally forced the government's hand and a Licences Reduction Board was set up to thin out the number of hotels.

To calculate what was an 'adequate' number of hotels for a neighbourhood, the board would consider its residential and working population and the nature of local industries. Some quarters of the city were found to have *seven times* the number deemed adequate. First to go were the rogues: pubs habitually found selling liquor on Sundays, serving 'disorderly persons' and so on. Next targeted were those that did the least business. The Royal Highlander was one of them. Most pubs on Flinders Street did a roaring trade from the docks and railways—but not this one.

In its place the headquarters of the Wharf Labourers' Union was built in 1916. During the bitter industrial disputes that followed the First World War, waterside workers would assemble here in their thousands, singing 'Solidarity' before marching on the docks or to Parliament House. With art nouveau stylings, porthole windows and a pair of life-sized bronze Viking ship prows jutting out high over Flinders Street, the Wharf Labourers' building stood out as an eccentric gem amid the bluestone bulk of the bond stores. When it was demolished in 1953, architect Robin Boyd mourned it as a true original. It was, he admitted, not really old and 'not even properly beautiful'; but,

> *In a city of façades based on or copied directly from those of Renaissance Italy, mediaeval England or pre-depression America, here was a building of strong individual character.*

On the opposite corner of Highlander Lane used to stand a massive bluestone bond store belonging to Cecilia Zander. When the Yarra rose in 1863, the only goods stored at submersible level in Zander's store were casks of spirits which bobbed, undamaged, on the floodwaters. Cecilia had inherited Zander's Bonded Stores on her husband's death in 1858 and carried on the business for forty years, expanding to six warehouses that stretched from Highlander Lane around the King Street corner. All had rear access from Highlander Lane, including one at 22 King Street that, in the 1970s, would be repurposed as The Underground: throbbing heart of Melbourne's disco scene. The raw industrial look set it apart from its King Street rival, Inflation, which looked Bee Gees white when spot-lit. (Both venues have since morphed into strip clubs.) The only bluestone building left standing in Highlander Lane was once part of Cecilia Zander's empire.

2:M

WATERSIDE HOTEL

CORNER FLINDERS & KING STREETS

Historically, the Waterside Hotel had a bloody reputation. Dock workers, union heavies and booze made for a pretty explosive cocktail. And, as an amenity to shiftworkers, pubs near the wharves could open at six in the morning—or even stay open all night—attracting all manner of blow-ins. Party people from the King Street nightclubs, closing just as the Waterside opened for the day, would add to the *frisson*. A coked-up boyfriend of mine once got himself a kicking here. Head, ribs, arm: nothing fatal.

It became the Waterside Hotel in 1915, after incarnations as the Mercantile, London & Carnarvon and even, briefly, the Duke of Edinburgh (a gesture of fealty on the occasion of Melbourne's first royal visit in 1867). As a flow-on from the efforts of the Licences Reduction Board, six o'clock closing of hotels was introduced in 1916. Smuggled in as a wartime measure, early closing wouldn't be rescinded for fifty years. The desperate ritual of the six o'clock swill—an entire evening's drinking crammed into the last few minutes before the bar closed—was probably as baleful as the prolonged sessions it replaced. Plus, six o'clock closing was blamed for making Melbourne a ghost town after dark. Even visitors staying in city hotels couldn't get a drink after six. Who could blame Ava Gardner if, during the filming of *On the Beach* in 1959, she said (though she denied it) that Melbourne was the ideal setting for a movie about the end of the world?

Step a short way along King Street and turn up Mercantile Place. A sign on the rear wall of the Waterside Hotel reads '6am till 6pm'—a relic of the six o'clock swill.

RAILWAY VIADUCT, WAILING WALL

CORNER FLINDERS & SPENCER STREETS

Right overhead is the curve of the infernal railway viaduct. Take a moment to look up, past the girdered, vaulted heft of the thing, to the almost whimsical filigree ironwork of the railings at the top. After taking the bend at Flinders Street, the elevated rail line finally touches down behind the grand pile of the former railway offices (now a hotel) here at the foot of Spencer Street. As best I can figure it, the viaduct abutment must rest on the last remaining stump of Batman's Hill.

This isn't the right spot to tell the story of Batman's Hill (see 2:P). For now, it's enough to know that it wasn't just Melbourne's first landmark, but the first to be wiped off the map. Or rather, Batman's Hill was uprooted by degrees and, each time, was pronounced *gone* and eulogised in sentimental terms. But no matter how many times 'the last' of it was dug away and pined over and redistributed across swamp and riverbank, a zombie remnant—always 'the last'—of the hill would subsequently be found and expunged in its turn.

For a long time, it's been accepted lore that 'the last' of Batman's Hill survived behind the brick wall that runs alongside the Flinders Street footpath here, starting under the viaduct and heading west. At the same time as the viaduct was built, in 1890, the straggling foot of Batman's Hill was cut away so that Flinders Street could be extended past Spencer, giving access to the docks and railway goods sheds. This finely engineered retaining wall of ornamental Hawthorn brick was built to hold back what remained of the hill.

Early in the twentieth century, a 'pick-up' system was introduced on Melbourne's docks. At the start of every shift, waterside workers had to assemble at the labour office, opposite here, and compete for a day's work. Union objections led to crippling strikes; afterwards, non-union labour and strike-breakers would be given preference at the pick-up. Those who missed out on work would congregate here, against the wall, to smoke and condole. They called it the Wailing Wall.

Ten panels of the wall were knocked down in 1999, for construction of Wurundjeri Way, an offshoot of the ring road. Now, the Melbourne Quarter (MQ) development has dug away the so-called 'last' remnant of Batman's Hill that the wall was built to retain. And, to facilitate 'a grand porte-cochere arrival experience', great holes have been punched through what remains of the Wailing Wall—a slight the developers passed off as 'restoration' ('for the first time, bluestone components of the wall will become publicly visible').

But the real 'last' of Batman's Hill surely survives, not just where the viaduct makes landfall but in the slope of Spencer Street as it rises to Collins. I mean, it's uphill. Ergo, it must be Batman's Hill.

2:0

RAILWAYS ADMINISTRATIVE OFFICES

SPENCER STREET, OPPOSITE FLINDERS LANE

During the boom decade of the 1880s, a tandem speculation in land *and* railways stretched suburban Melbourne far and wide. The Railway Department's administrative offices were here: built, along with the viaduct and other large-scale works, just before the boom collapsed into depression. The 'palatial' scale of the railway offices, in particular, drew scorn in the lean years that followed, resulting in the dismissal of the railway commissioners.

As well as a boardroom bigger than a parliamentary chamber, the building featured thirty-two 'automatic sanitary closets' with deodorising flush mechanisms and self-closing lids. Right above the main entrance were three sculpted female figures, goddess types in classical robes. Two of them were seated, contemplating the progress of science and the arts, while between them towered triumphant Liberty, wings spread and torch aloft. The sculptor, John Mackennal, worked from a studio at the far end of Collins Street, beside Howitt's old garden. (See 1:F.) Another commission of his was the happy farm animals on the pediment of the meat hall at Queen Vic Market. (See 7:C.)

2:P

BATMAN'S HILL

COLLINS STREET & WURUNDJERI WAY

What a complicated, unnatural spot this is.

Railyards and goods sheds used to cover the ground beneath this bridge and spread westward towards the docks that gave Docklands its name. To make way for them, the hill that stood here—Batman's Hill—had been 'cut down'. Cutting down a tree is one thing; but cutting down a hill?

Its Kulin name went unrecorded, but the very first Melburnians, Johnny Fawkner's party, called it Pleasant Hill. John Batman claimed the hill and built his house on the slope facing the river. Fawkner would complain that it was by 'toadyism'—gifts of milk and eggs to government officials—that Batman got the hill named after him. (Fawkner was always happy to share his supplies, but *never* gratis.) A rounded knoll dotted with sheoaks, Batman's Hill offered a natural vantage point from which to take in the growing town.

Early on, all the government stores and offices, the court, gaol and military barracks were quartered at this end of town. (See 6:Q.) Following Batman's death in 1839, his house became Melbourne's first treasury building. When Robert Hoddle surveyed the site of Melbourne in 1837, he took the summit of Batman's Hill as its datum point: all distances were measured from there. The hill itself was reserved for a botanic gardens. Part of it was fenced and planted with indigenous and exotic trees; on summer evenings the military band played there. But as the town developed eastwards, Batman's Hill fell off the map. Hemmed on three sides by the river and swamp land, it came to mark Melbourne's western margin. When a new botanic gardens site was reserved at South Yarra, the former beauty spot became a dumping ground. Gunpowder and explosives were stored there,* tents were put up for the quarantine of smallpox patients, and what had been envisaged as 'one of the pleasantest promenades in the environs of the city' became a favourite resort of vagrants. Batman's Hill lost its prominence—first figuratively, then literally.

The first incursion came in 1855, when tunnels were bored through the hill for pipes to bring gas to the town from the gasworks, on the Docklands side of the hill. Inside, the hill was honeycombed with wombat burrows and the tunnellers found fossilised tree trunks, 'meteoric' iron and

* Hence Gunpowder Walk, part of the sprawling MQ development.

quartz flecked with gold. By 1863, the whole of the hill had been handed over for railway purposes and the work of 'removing' Batman's Hill began.

'Batman's-hill is now almost a thing of the past…' As part of the levelling works, Batman's old house was to be demolished, prompting the first stirrings of something like heritage consciousness. Batman's house was 'perhaps, the only valuable relic of the kind we possess in Melbourne'—

> *Let any one stand on the hill behind this house, let him cast his eyes over the great city before him that has sprung up within the last thirty years…Where else will be found a spot more suggestive, or one that for the sake of our children we ought to guard with more jealous care.*

But, after all, the house had stood there for just twenty-eight years and, as a more bloodless Melburnian wrote—

> *It is a universal circumstance attending the growth of a rapidly developing city, that it speedily effaces the last few lingering memorials of its origin. Their date is so recent they are looked upon as eyesores and obstructions before they have endured sufficiently long to have become respectable by their age…We cannot afford to let the past act as an obstruction to the present. Let the hill go…*

Bit by bit, they did. In the 1870s, sites were levelled for

freight sheds 'formed out of the excavation of Batman's-hill, the last trace of which has now disappeared'. Then, in preparation for the 'railway extravagance' of the early 1890s, fugitive remnants were found to be still in need of removal. 'When the last of it has gone, the oldest landmark in Melbourne will have gone with it, and Batman's Hill will only be known in history.' Clay and gravel from the hill didn't travel far, but were used to fill in the swamp, for the levelling of Spencer Street and to shore up the banks of the Yarra.

The construction of the bridge you're standing on, as part of Collins Street's extension into Docklands in 2003, went some way towards reinstating Batman's Hill. Bruce Armstrong's sculpture *Eagle*—inspired by the Kulin creator-spirit, Bunjil—was raised around that same time, to survey the lost hill from on high. And not far from here, in the direction of the river, a pole was put up to mark the location and elevation (eighteen metres) of the hill's summit, as well as Hoddle's datum point.* Standing here, then, you'd have been on the northern slope of Batman's Hill which (turn around!) in 1838 served as grandstand for Melbourne's first racecourse, laid out on the flat.

* The pole isn't visible now, but may yet reappear as part of the ongoing MQ development planned for the site. For now, the new Sky Park at One MQ (699 Bourke Street)—just over the bridge and up sixty-six spiral stairs (or by elevator)—gives you the nearest approximation of Batman's hilltop.

Remember I called this an unnatural spot, this apology for a hill? Well, the further you head into Docklands, the more unnatural things get. Unnatural, at least, to anyone who knew this place before. Hold that thought.

2:Q

WEST MELBOURNE SWAMP, NO. 2 GOODS SHED

YELLOW-TOPPED WALL BESIDE 700 COLLINS STREET

To anyone who knew this place before...Before Docklands, before the railways, before the smallpox tents or the racecourse or John Batman, the view from here was of wetlands. Teeming with waterfowl—ducks, swans, geese, plover, snipe, curlews, quails, ibis, gulls, cormorants—this was a place of abundance. Part of the marshy expanse that separated the Yarra and Maribyrnong rivers, it was also a dividing zone between Woiwurrung- and Boonwurrung-speaking clans. Their countries converged here.

The people who displaced them would come shooting here for breakfast. They first called these wetlands a lagoon or lake, before downgrading it to a swamp, either Batman's or the West Melbourne. Its appearance in springtime—'a real lake, intensely blue, nearly oval, and full of the clearest salt water'—earned it the name the Blue Lake. Fringed about with golden myrniong flowers and the magenta blaze of pigface, it would be remembered as 'one of the chief beauty-spots' of the young town. Pretty soòn, though, it was only a memory, as the effluent of North and West Melbourne drained into the swamp and cattle were put there to graze. Most Melburnians came to regard these wetlands (if they thought of them at all) as an obstacle to the city's westward expansion.

From as early as 1841, there were calls to drain 'the dismal swamp of Batman' and progressively, from the 1870s, it happened. Drainage channels were cut, the Yarra's lower course was altered and, from 1886, the Coode Canal led ships to Victoria Dock, a deep anchorage where brolgas had once waded. Railyards and dockyards stretched to meet one another across the land reclaimed, in part, by the conglomeration of Batman's hill with his swamp.

> *The commercial and manufacturing growth and increase of our city demand that facilities should be afforded for its extension in a westerly direction.*

That was written in 1872, but a hundred-plus years later capitalists were still talking that way. The hill and the swamp were gone, but Melbourne still stopped short at Spencer Street. The obstacle now was the railways: Spencer Street station and its sprawl of railyards and shedding. Right below where you're standing is the northern half of the No. 2 goods shed (there used to be six of them) which, at 385 metres long, was once Australia's longest building. (Go on, take the stairs down and circumnavigate it.) Despite its heritage listing, this string bean of bricks was sliced in two when Collins Street was extended and Docklands created in the 2000s. *Westward, ho!*

It's not just the re-re-engineering of the landscape that makes me call Docklands unnatural. No, mine is a fundamentally Melbourne objection. You know about Hoddle's grid, all those right angles pivoting off a precise spot on Batman's Hill? And of course, because it's a grid, Collins and Bourke streets run parallel, right? Not anymore. Take a tram west from here and you'll arrive at *the intersection of Collins and Bourke streets.* Talk about a mind-fuck. Welcome to Docklands.

2:R

WEEPING WOMAN

LITTLE COLLINS STREET, NEAR SPENCER STREET

Steps here used to lead down to a subway from which, on the other side of Spencer Street, ramps led up to the train platforms. Along the subway walls were ranks of coin-fed luggage lockers of gunmetal grey, each with a number stencilled in gold. As a country train-traveller of a book-buying disposition, I used those lockers a lot.

The National Gallery of Victoria paid $1.6 million in 1985 for its (then) highest-priced acquisition, Picasso's *Weeping Woman*. When the painting was discovered missing from its frame a year later, responsibility was claimed by the hitherto-and-since-unheard-of Australian Cultural Terrorists. Ransom demands called for an increase in government funding for the arts, plus an annual art prize (neither was forthcoming). After two weeks came a tip-off, and the Picasso was found safe in locker number 227 in the Spencer Street subway. Police dusted the locker door but found it 'too greasy' to yield fingerprints. The culprits were never found; nor was their trophy, the key to locker 227.

Ten years later, those old lockers were replaced by electronic ones, with instructions supplied by a talking parrot. A few years more and, as part of the Docklands scheme, Spencer Street station itself was replaced by the ripple-roofed Southern Cross station—commonly misheard as Southern Crustacean and hence the Crab Shack.

This convenient subway entrance closed when the old station went, though rumours of its reopening have surfaced from time to time. There are still luggage lockers at Southern Cross station—but good luck finding one that works.

WALK 3

MORE BY LAND THAN WATER

In which we weave through Theatre-land, Chinatown and the 'back slums', with guest appearances by Joe Cocker and the ghost of James Brown

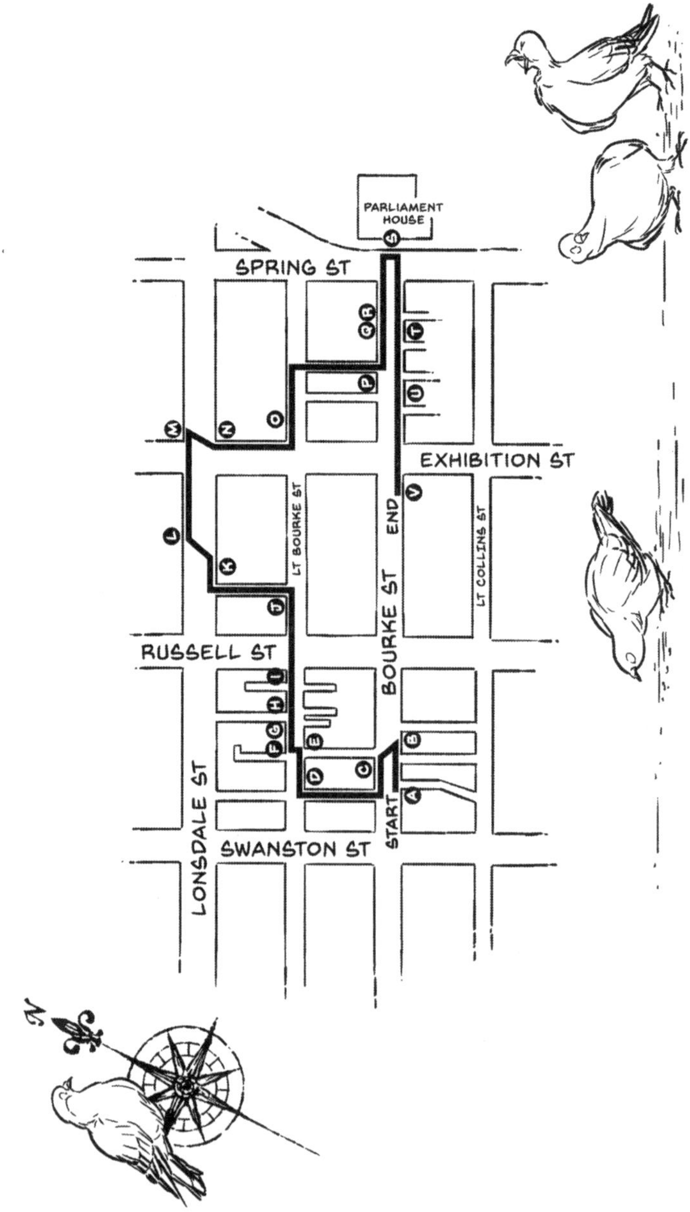
PARLIAMENT HOUSE
SPRING ST
EXHIBITION ST
RUSSELL ST
SWANSTON ST
LONSDALE ST
LT BOURKE ST
BOURKE ST
LT COLLINS ST
START
END

3:A

CAFÉ CLAIRVOYANTS

TIVOLI ARCADE, BOURKE STREET

The Tivoli Theatre, on this spot, was the toe-tip of the Bourke Street theatre district. Any Saturday night between the 1850s and the First World War, Bourke Street east of here was 'a flaring city canyon that seethed with life'. Saturday was payday, and this was where waged-up Melburnians came for amusement: besides theatres, there were waxworks and freak shows, 'sporty' hotels, Paddy's Market and no end of wily touts and magsmen with tricks in their waistcoat pockets. At times, there were as many as six theatres operating along this stretch from Swanston to Russell Street, serving up opera, Shakespeare, minstrelsy and arithmetical pigs. Some of the theatres, rejigged to show movies, would linger on through the twentieth century. But the Tivoli survived as a vestige of vaudeville until the 1960s, so there are performers still working who had their start at 'the Tiv'.

The Tivoli Café, on the downhill side of the theatre entrance, was one of several city cafés targeted in 1932 by a police blitz on fortune-telling. As a lure to customers during the pinched times of the Depression, some cafés were offering palm readings along with refreshments. A squad of plain-clothes police staged a sting at three Bourke Street cafés in one afternoon. At the Tivoli Café two policewomen ordered 'pineapple specials' and paid an extra sixpence each for a reading. *Bam!* Proprietor Denes Raftopoulos was sprung, and charged under the Police Offences Act.

A few doors uphill, the Royal Café—run by Raftopoulos's uncle, George Black (né Gerasimos Mavromates)—was raided the same afternoon. There, the policewomen ordered ice cream and had their palms read by a Madame Valda. Constable Betty Martin went first. 'You have a very sensitive hand,' observed Madame Valda. 'You are easily hurt, and will travel more by land than by water. If you are not married, you will be.' And she added, 'Do you know any one named Arthur?' The sitter replied in the affirmative, and Madame Valda turned to the hand of Constable Lily Smith. 'You will have an operation, but not for some time. You will live until seventy-eight, and if you are not married you will be. You will meet someone who has an aeroplane and will go exploring and suffer from headaches.'

As plain Valda Wingrove, Madame V would testify in court that she had taught herself palmistry and crystal-gazing from a book after her husband lost his job and, though she gave about twenty readings a day, she was paid only the going rate for a waitress. The question of illegality hinged on whether customers were 'imposed upon' by her predictions. She admitted that of course she couldn't tell how long Constable Smith would live; but she always warned customers not to take her readings seriously.

Besides, as her lawyer said, surely the two policewomen had 'received their money's worth in amusement'.

Victoria's Chief Secretary (whose name *was* Arthur) would explicitly ban fortune-telling the following year, insisting that 'many women reacted adversely' to predictions like Madame Valda's. The prohibition against 'Fortune Telling and Pretending to Exercise Witchcraft, etc.' would remain on the books until 2005.

3:B

PALACE HOTEL

225 BOURKE STREET (CORNER RUSSELL PLACE)

Caged in the backyard tea garden of the City Buffet Hotel, on this spot, were a pair of lions named Wallace and Lola, an Indian bear, a cheetah, some monkeys and an aviary of songbirds.

It wasn't uncommon to see exotic animals served up as a hotel sideshow. They could be got cheaply from a disbanding circus or travelling animal show and—*voila!*—who needed a billiard table? One Adelaide hotel had *an elephant* in its beer garden. The City Buffet menagerie would eventually be offered to the Victorian Acclimatisation Society as the basis for the zoological collection that would grow into the Melbourne Zoo.

LOLA WALLACE

Replacing the City Buffet in 1876 was the Academy of Music—actually a theatre, showcasing music and drama 'in their higher manifestations'. The décor was suitably classical in tone: tessellated floors, statues on pedestals. In the glass-roofed Victoria Arcade, adjoining, the Orchestrion, an enormous clockwork mechanism 'with the powers of a full band', played at intervals through the day.

Artiste-in-residence for the Academy's premier season was the European coloratura soprano Ilma de Murska. As an entourage, she brought along a cat, a monkey, a pair of parrots and her beloved Newfoundland dog, Pluto. Unlike Wallace and Lola, Mademoiselle de Murska's companions roamed free, the cat and monkey squabbling, the parrots shredding the furniture and Pluto seated beside his mistress at dinner.

With a capacity of 'only' 1,500, the Academy of Music was considered a modest-sized theatre for Melbourne. In time, its name would change to the Bijou and its bill of fare to comedy. Here, in 1879, was staged *The Happy Land*, Marcus Clarke's burlesque on colonial politics, so scandalous that the government tried to suppress it 'on the grounds of morality'. Performances went ahead, but whenever an actor came to a redacted passage, they'd give a significant cough and darkly intone, '*Cen-sored!*'

Alongside the Bijou Theatre, in 1889, arose the majestic new Palace Hotel. Seven storeys high, it had 250 rooms, all with hot and cold water, speaking tubes and electric light laid on. In the vast kitchen (the steam-heated carving table alone was more than ten metres long), cunningly arranged mirrors ensured that food preparation was hidden from diners' view. The public rooms and vestibules were painted with frescoed scenes from Shakespeare and the novels of Sir Walter Scott. The Palace had hydraulic elevators, its own aerated water plant and, on the roof, a roller-skating rink!

Not long after the Palace Hotel's opening, fire destroyed the Bijou Theatre. The Palace was merely singed on that occasion, but over the following year it would survive *eight* deliberately lit fires. Four were started in the space of just one night; three of them in locked and empty bedrooms. Was the place haunted? The owner of the Palace was beside himself: no company would insure the hotel and no one wanted to stay there. He hired firemen to patrol the hotel at night, offered a reward for information leading to the culprit and paid for an inquiry to be held by Dr Youl, the coroner. Youl's initial surmise was that the arsonist must be 'a woman afflicted with fire disease', since any man wishing to burn the hotel down would, he reasoned, have succeeded on the first attempt. Eventually, though, the finger *did* point to a man: Oswald Twist, the hotel's night-porter, whose job it was to roam the hotel corridors collecting guests' boots for cleaning and who, when a fire started, seemed never to be far away. Twist was duly arrested and tried but escaped conviction, thanks to a welter of perjurious witnesses vying for the reward.

3:C

THEATRE ROYAL / COLES DEPARTMENT STORE

236 BOURKE STREET (KMART)

Being burnt to the ground was practically a rite of passage for a theatre in the nineteenth century. (Newspaper compositors could set the phrase *phoenix from the ashes* in type with their eyes closed.) It happened to the Theatre Royal, on this spot, in 1872. George Coppin, Melbourne's foremost theatrical entrepreneur, was staging the melodrama *Streets of New York*, whose sensational Act V called for a raging tenement fire, with real flames. Asking for trouble, you would think.

The Theatre Royal had been launched here in 1855 on the rollicking wave of gold-rush prosperity. Early on, Lola Montez and her Spider Dance ('utterly subversive to all ideas of public morality') lost the theatre any claim to respectability, and the fifty-metre-long bar off the vestibule became a popular rendezvous for prostitutes and their customers, earning it the nickname the Saddling Paddock. Coppin took over the Theatre Royal in 1856 and, to offset the riff-raffishness, added the Café de Paris next door.

Palatial and elegant, roofed with a stained-glass dome, the Café was Melbourne's classiest eating house. Saving it from stuffiness was its genial and bohemian host, Christopher

Pond, who was also maestro of the gigantic grid-iron where diners could watch their meat being grilled to perfection. (See 3:Q.) With his Café de Paris business partner, Felix Spiers, Pond sponsored the first Australian tour of the English cricket team and even tried to lure Charles Dickens into a literary tour of the colonies. Leaving for England in 1863, the pair was soon running refreshment rooms at railway stations from Dover to Newcastle. With restaurants in London's West End and hotels all over England, Pond and Spiers would end up the world's pre-eminent caterers.

In the twentieth century, department stores and cinemas came to dominate this stretch of Bourke Street. The Theatre Royal was swept away in 1933 for the six-storey art deco Manton's, 'a 100 per cent daylight store' (whatever that meant). On the ground floor, the former location of the Theatre Royal stage was marked by a plaque with a time capsule behind it, containing a brick from the old theatre and...what else? A call went out for suggestions of objects typifying present-day Melbourne life. Submissions included: a factory whistle, an embalmed politician, a car horn, a powder compact and lipstick, and (most popular) a bottle of whisky.

A Coles department store replaced Manton's in 1955. This was Coles' second CBD store. The first, just one block down (opposite Myer), had opened in 1930 and was the

Australian pioneer of the in-store cafeteria. Occupying an entire floor, with seating for a thousand and a truck-sized dishwasher fed by conveyor belt, Coles' cafeteria was an operation rivalling anything Pond and Spiers could have dreamed up. Diners slid stainless-steel trays along steel grilles to select meals from bain maries and shelves of plated sandwiches and desserts in parfait glasses. The noise—'the prolonged / Crash of the Cafeterias at noon'*—was something tremendous. The new store on the Theatre Royal site would double Coles' Bourke Street cafeteria capacity just in time for the Olympics.

Because this Coles store was flanked by cinemas when I was a kid, it was always here that we'd have lunch when we came to 'town' for a school-holiday treat: stras sandwiches, a milkshake or spider and a bowl of jelly. Memorably, my brother spewed lime spider over a woman's white fur coat on our way from Coles' cafeteria to see *Chitty Chitty Bang Bang*. Maybe ten years later, when I was a student at RMIT, we'd congregate after class…where else but Coles' cafeteria. Stainless-steel pots of tea, neenish tarts, the same old prolonged crash. I dare say we imagined ourselves Warholian iconoclasts (I wore a watch around one ankle) but really, it was nice there among the nannas.

* From Furnley Maurice's poem, 'Melbourne and Memory', 1934.

3:D

THEATRE ROYAL STAGE ENTRANCE
205 LITTLE BOURKE STREET

Here was the Theatre Royal's stage door, built wide enough to admit stage props and the fire brigade as well as livestock, which would occasionally form part of the entertainment—like the horses that were ridden down Little Bourke Street at a gallop, through the doorway here and onto the stage for a crowd-pleasing finish at the footlights. Only once did a rider lose his grip on the reins and topple into the orchestra pit. Two of George Coppin's own horses, Mirth and Music, featured in a production in the 1880s. Before they were his, they'd belonged to Ned Kelly and Joe Byrne: the horses were seized by police after the Kelly gang's doomed siege at Glenrowan and bought by Coppin at auction.

Early one Saturday in 1859, a Bengal tiger named Hercules escaped from his enclosure at the rear of Wombwell's Zoological Exhibition, next to the Theatre Royal. In one sense, no one was surprised: Hercules had been roaring and restless ever since he arrived from Singapore. But for the men who slept above a Chinese grocer's store opposite, 'surprised' would have been putting it mildly. Finding a rear door open, the liberated Hercules ransacked the shop before climbing the stairs to the living quarters and mauling the shoulder of one of the sleeping men.

Also penned up at Wombwell's were three leopards and a six-metre crocodile, along with the lions, Wallace and Lola (namesake of the Theatre Royal's first headlining act), in their original Melbourne home. (See 3:B.)

3:E

CHINESE QUARTER
LA TROBE PLACE

This was formerly Davis Lane—which means that C. J. La Trobe, the epaulette-wearing first governor of Victoria, ranks with AC/DC as a street-name usurper. True, Davis the saddler was long gone by the time the lane was renamed, circa 1885. But so was La Trobe.

The reason for the renaming seems to have been the usual one: to sweeten a sullied locale.

> *Within a stone's throw of Bourke-street are places where the most ordinary hygienic laws are completely ignored, where overcrowded dilapidated houses can be counted by the hundred—squalid, noisome regions, the abodes or rather lairs of men and women who have abandoned themselves to immorality and crime.*

The laneways and rights-of-way off Little Bourke Street East had been the focus of an 1883 enquiry into 'the condition of the dwellings and the circumstances of the inhabitants in the "back slums" of Melbourne', with Davis Lane singled out as one of the worst. The Theatre Royal's George Coppin was a member of the committee of enquiry and, running for parliament that same year, he pitched himself as 'the originator of the present popular movement to improve the back slums of Melbourne...which must greatly increase the value of property in those localities'.

The enquiry would denounce the landlords who profited mightily from the rents of substandard shacks—some made from rickety packing cases, none with proper plumbing or drainage—that crammed the offshoots of Little Bourke. Bluestone-cobbled laneways were ankle deep in festering garbage and sewage from overflowing (or non-existent) privies. In Davis Lane and *its* offshoots (yes, there were rights-of-way off the rights-of-way) the back-slums investigators found rooms too squat to stand up in, roofs like sieves, stagnant water pooling under floors, dampness and mould on every surface, and privies in kitchens and on front verandahs.

Should we be surprised to learn that the landlord of five such houses alongside the Theatre Royal in Davis Lane was none other than George Coppin? And that all his tenants were Chinese?

When Chinese in their thousands joined the gold rush to Victoria in 1854, the colony had responded with alarm and hostility, levying a heavy tax on each new arrival from China as a deterrent. Even so, by 1856, there were an estimated twenty-five thousand Chinese in Victoria, mostly men and nearly all of them on the goldfields. But some two hundred of the new immigrants had settled in Melbourne and already 'that portion of Little Bourke street between Swanston and Russell streets displays all the characteristics of a Chinese quarter'. Melbourne's Chinese community would grow over the next twenty years in inverse proportion to diminishing prospects on the goldfields, until the Chinese quarter stretched up Little Bourke and its branching alleyways, nearly all the way to Spring Street.

3:F

LOTTERY SHOPS
CELESTIAL AVENUE

At a time when China was known in the west as the Celestial Empire, it followed that its citizens were Celestials and that, in the heart of Melbourne's Chinatown, a street should be given that name. For twenty years this was Celestial Alley; only in the pretentious 1880s was it uplifted to *Avenue.*

There were traders and craftsmen in Chinatown as enterprising and skilful as you'd find anywhere in the city. But, let's be honest: the Chinese quarter was home to a great many displaced and lonely men (expatriate Chinese women were relatively few). To fill the void, gambling, opium-smoking and prostitution flourished, contributing to the debauched and squalid reputation of Little Bourke Street East.

Fan-tan (a game played with tiles) was the favoured flutter of Melbourne's Chinese themselves. But lotteries run by Chinese syndicates in Little Bourke Street caught on among non-Chinese. This was the ancient game of *baige piao*—the origin of keno, lotto and bingo—in which a player marked ten out of eighty numbers on a ticket for a one-in-8.9-million chance of a big win. In 1892, the police mounted a campaign against the 'rampant Chinese lottery evil', raiding ticket shops all through the Chinese quarter.

Quang Mow Shang, ostensibly a tea merchant, kept a lottery shop at the corner of Davis Lane, opposite. (He was a tenant of George Coppin's.) When the police swooped around midnight on a Saturday the place was packed with ticket buyers while Quang Mow Shang reclined on a divan, toking on a gold-mounted opium pipe. Based on cash found on the premises, police estimated the lottery shop's weekly takings at £300—equal to an annual wage for many at the time.

That same night, police raided a heavily guarded building at the far end of Celestial Avenue, exposing a lottery syndicate's 'bank'. At the rear of an old bluestone hall facing Lonsdale Street—lately a masonic lodge—a series of rooms had been 'fitted up in an extraordinary manner'. Opening onto a narrow passageway were nine chambers, each sealed by wooden doors that slid back to reveal an iron grille. Inside were piles and piles of lottery tickets.

Evidently this was where the lotteries were drawn, and the presence in each room of two 'formidable' machete-like knives suggested both the integrity of the draw and that money must be stored here somewhere. In 'secret safes', police surmised, though no such safe was found. Where did all the lottery money go?

3:G

SAM YUP CLUBHOUSE

200–202 LITTLE BOURKE STREET

The Sam Yup (Three Districts) and See Yup (Four Districts) societies were founded in Melbourne in 1854 for the cultural, corporeal and spiritual support of gold-rush immigrants from Guangdong province in southern China. Merchant Lowe Kong Meng—wealthy, cultured and fluent in four languages—was among the first of his countrymen to put down roots in Little Bourke Street. As president of the Sam Yup Society,* in 1861 he commissioned this fine building, variously referred to as a clubhouse, courthouse, lodging-house and 'Chinese Exchange'. Perhaps the word

* The Sam Yup Society would later become the Num Pon Soon Society.

that suits it best is *huikuan*, a kind of assembly hall used for a range of functions, including worship. (One room is dedicated to a shrine honouring ancestors.)

But the Sam Yup building was first announced as 'a court-house, where disputes amongst Chinamen will be disposed of after their own manner and according to their own laws'. On the goldfields, some temples (or 'joss houses') served the same role. Chinese parties in dispute usually sought justice through their community's own arbitration court; only if dissatisfied with the outcome would they take their complaint to the police or mainstream courts of law. It sounds like a decent stab at self-governance by a diaspora, but critics of the system argued—with what justification?—that community arbitration gave 'secret societies' undue power over vulnerable Chinese immigrants.

3:H

KEM WAH'S WORKSHOP

HEFFERNAN LANE

A much-admired feature of the See Yup temple built at South Melbourne in 1866 were its intricately carved and gilded traditional wooden screens and altars. They were created on this spot, in the workshop of carpenter Kem Wah. Carved from kauri and huon pine, they depicted elaborate scenes of battle and reconciliation, all executed 'with that minute labour-loving accuracy of detail which gives such a character to Chinese art'. Carvings from Kem Wah's workshop were shown at the Intercolonial Exhibition held in Melbourne in 1867, as an example of 'the artistic capabilities of the Chinese portion of our population'.

Chinese carpentry of a different kind would come to dominate Little Bourke Street and its tributaries from the 1870s onwards. Cabinetmaking workshops sprang up in every alley and laneway, manufacturing inexpensive household furniture: chairs, wardrobes, chests of drawers. By the 1890s one-tenth of Victorian Chinese were employed in such workshops, and non-Chinese furniture makers protested that their cheap labour made for unfair competition. In the run-up to Federation, the same racial antagonism that gave rise to the White Australia Policy led to laws requiring that Chinese cabinetmakers stamp their products Made By Chinese Labour.

Also plentiful in the Chinese quarter were fruit wholesalers, many of them dealing solely in Queensland bananas. In 1900 there were *seven* banana merchants within a stone's throw of here.

3:1

'BROGANS LANE' / EXFORD HOTEL
WARATAH PLACE

This used to be Williams Lane, and before that it was the disreputable Brogans Lane—or was it? For decades from the 1850s, it was marked as Brogans Lane on maps and directories, but press reports of depraved goings-on in 'that malodorous region' often clearly referred to a different lane, further up Bourke Street. Eventually the picture cleared: *this* was Williams, *that* was Brogans (that is, until it wasn't). We'll arrive there shortly; but, for now, think of this as the *phantom* Brogans Lane.

The Exford Hotel is a survivor. Here since the 1850s, it's been substantially rebuilt at least twice, most recently in the early twentieth century, when it got those leadlight windows. The cellar was cleared out at that time and, in a recess under the footpath, workmen found an old bricked-up oven. Inside were fifty fluted bottles of ruinously vintage champagne. In a spirit of experiment one was uncorked, releasing a toxic cloud of mist. No one was game to try so much as a sip.

3:J

THE REAL BROGANS LANE

CORRS LANE

So, this was the *real* Brogans Lane: the lane the *Herald* once called 'a plague spot on our social existence, which will do more harm than would a thousand men like Kelly riding the bush red-handed'. Ned Kelly, at the time, was wanted for the murder of three policemen at Stringybark Creek. That's how bad Brogans Lane was.

Its tenements, crammed into a warren of yards and alleys, were owned by the widow of Patrick Brogan, after whom the lane was named. 'While the late Mr Brogan lived,' said the *Herald*, 'he allowed none of the houses in the lane to be tenanted to loose women; but his widow encourages such tenants.' She collected rent from something like twenty 'hovels' in Brogans Lane.

In 1883, the back-slums enquiry condemned the lane as 'shockingly bad and filthy' and a 'hotbed of vice'. Most of the tenants were Chinese men, some with European 'consorts'. They lived in rooms hardly more than two metres square, with ceilings high enough only for stooping. Wastewater draining down from Lonsdale Street mixed with the lane's own effluent to form putrid pools. A walking stick poked into a hole in the floor of one dwelling revealed a stagnant accumulation of 'water, mud and slime' two feet (60 cm) deep. Given that there was 'little or no closet accommodation' in Brogans Lane (not wardrobes, of course, but toilets), the back-slums inspectors expressed amazement 'that the occupants are so free from fevers and sickness':

> *Opium appears to have some peculiar disinfectant property. At all events it is death to vermin and, in all the dirt and filth throughout Little Bourke-street, fleas are unknown.*

I say that this was the real Brogans Lane, yet for years it masqueraded as Carrs or Corrs while, on the books, it was the lane behind the Exford Hotel that bore the name Brogans *and* the opprobrium of newspaper readers. But this was the lane, for certain, where Mrs Brogan collected her rents and neglected her responsibilities. In only one year, 1880, did the city directories set the record straight, exposing *this* as the despised Brogans Lane. An outbreak of seemliness brought on by that year's Melbourne Exhibition led to a program of civic cleansing (more nomenclative than substantive) and, officially at least, Brogans Lane ceased to exist.

*Un*officially though, in Melbourne lore, Brogans Lane lived on. The press would continue to invoke it, right up till the First World War, as the last two words in depravity. And Louis Esson made a poem of it, that began, *There's a crack in the city*...and ended, *The river and morgue shadow Brogans Lane.*

For a city-snoop, the best thing about Corrs Lane is the skinny brick passage at its northern end. Ducking into it from Lonsdale Street feels like disappearing down *a crack in the city*, and emerging from it is like...well, see for yourself.

3:K

CHATEAU COMMODORE

131 LONSDALE STREET (HOTEL GRAND CHANCELLOR)

In 1972, Melbourne radio station 3AK tried to wrest the youth audience off its rival, 3XY, by branding itself *3AK: Where No Wrinklys Fly*. Ads in *Go-Set* and on posters around town featured a giant prune (caption: 'A wrinkly is a guy who pretends he's your uncle when he's really looking down your dress') and a Brady-Bunch grid of images—Janis Joplin, a peace sign, a black man holding a white baby, Che Guevara, a naked hippy couple, a dune buggy, a modular plastic chair—above the words: 'If you turned up your nose once, you're a wrinkly.' A wrinkly was the boomers' boomer.

Another icon pictured in that wrinkly-test grid was Joe Cocker. Touring Australia in 1972—three years after his electrifying performance at Woodstock—he was convicted in Adelaide of marijuana possession. Cocker's next stop was Melbourne and he stayed here, at what was then the Chateau Commodore Hotel. During his first Festival Hall gig, Cocker chugged bottles of whisky and champagne before throwing his sandshoes and T-shirt into the audience. Later, when he reeled into the Chateau Commodore, barefoot and shirtless, the manager demanded he leave. Cocker made to lob a can of Foster's and was tackled by a plainclothes policeman, triggering a slugfest that, with the arrival of police reinforcements, progressed from the casino-style carpet of the hotel lobby out onto the street. Backing singers, roadies, girlfriends—the whole entourage joined in the melée. Cocker was held overnight in the Russell Street police cells while the federal government moved to have him deported.

Next day his support band would act as decoys, leaving for the airport with jackets over their heads while Cocker was smuggled to Festival Hall for his last show. (The promoters took a punt that federal police wouldn't seize him once he was on stage.) That night on ATV-0, Melbourne's newest TV channel, Cocker was lambasted as 'another one of those uncouth, dirty-haired, sloppily dressed show-business freaks…who because of overnight fame and pure disregard for what normal people regard as decent behaviour has decided that Australia is the sort of outpost where he can indulge in his filthy habits'. Cocker, meanwhile, made a parting prediction that within five years marijuana would be legal in Australia and 'the cat who is trying to throw us out now will be smoking it himself'.

If he wasn't exactly right, he wasn't far wrong. In Australia, 1972 was epochal. It was the year of the first Sunbury rock festival. The taboo-busting TV soap *Number 96* made its debut. My high school, when the year began, was still policing hemlines and regulation bloomers; by term four they'd given up. And six weeks after Cocker's last Melbourne show, Gough Whitlam would replace Billy McMahon as prime minister. As for 3AK...well, talk about bucking the trend. In 1973 it didn't just give up its bid for the youth market but went full wrinkly, adopting a Beautiful Music format—wall-to-wall Mantovani—that was the aural equivalent of the Chateau Commodore carpet *before* Joe Cocker scuffed its pile.

In a neat cultural conjunction, the Chateau Commodore would go on to play itself in *The Box*, ATV-0's attempt to out-raunch *Number 96*. Launched in 1974, *The Box* was set at a fictional Melbourne TV station whose pansexual on-screen talent and adulterous execs indulged *their* filthy habits, after hours, at the classy local watering-hole: you guessed it, the Chateau Commodore.

3:L

PRINCESS MARY CLUB
130 LONSDALE STREET

Here stood the Princess Mary Club, a hostel for country girls working or studying in Melbourne. Built in 1926 by the Wesley Central Mission (with money from a pharmaceutical magnate) the club aimed to shelter young women from the city's undesirable influences. But while other church-sponsored hostels were inclined to be preachy and parsimonious, the Princess Mary Club was ecumenical, lenient and almost luxurious. For a bargain thirty shillings a week, a boarder got a comfortably furnished bedroom and three meals daily. There were baths and even showers (almost unheard of then) on each floor and, downstairs, a sumptuous lounge complete with grand piano *and* pianola. As for rules, 'All we ask of the girls who come to live with us,' said the club's matron, 'is that they will behave just as they would in their own homes.'

By the time I came to know it, the Princess Mary Club had pretty much outlived its original function. In the mid-1980s, accompanied by that rarest of creatures, a boyfriend who loved to dance, I took Latin American dancing lessons in a big room (was it the lounge?) on the ground floor. We stuck at it only long enough to master the cha-cha. But—what bliss. We'd leave that hall glowing.

In front of the Princess Mary Club was a compact lawn

set behind a hedge. It was a tiny oasis in the concrete city and at lunchtime office workers would come in off the street and lounge on the grass in the sun.* I'd lounge here myself when I worked at this end of town, girl-fridaying on an archaeological dig.

The Princess Mary Club closed in 1990, after which it was home only to pigeons. When it was demolished nearly thirty years later, archaeologists excavating the site were surprised to find substantial remains of earlier buildings way below present-day street level. There must originally have been a dip in the ground here: when Melbourne was being hurriedly remade to meet the exigencies of the gold rush, property owners were ordered to build up low-lying land to match the newly established street level. In some cases, houses were simply abandoned and then clay, rubbish, whatever, was piled over the top. In 2017, archaeologists found brick and stone walls and fireplaces—entire skeletons of early houses—still standing, 'Pompei-like', deep underground.

Never imagining what lay beneath, back in 1988 I lunched on the Princess Mary Club lawn with a friend who was roadie-ing for AC/DC. They were in town with their Blow

* A grassy oasis can now be found at the rear of the church, facing Bennetts Lane (see 4:H).

Up Your Video tour and were billeted at the Rockman's Regency (now the Marriott), just up the street. I half expected to hear of Cocker-worthy hijinks. But no. Angus and the lads, it seemed, spent their downtime playing golf. And why not? By then Joe Cocker had been back to Australia several times without threat of expulsion. More a balladeer now than a brawler, he probably played golf on his days off too.

3:M

'SYRIAN' QUARTER

CORNER LONSDALE & EXHIBITION STREETS

For decades, beginning in the 1880s, this was the heart of Melbourne's 'Syrian' quarter. Uphill along Lonsdale Street and northwards on Exhibition many of the occupants had names like Haddad, Maloof, Bacash, Ameer, Habib and Khaled. Most of them we'd recognise today as Lebanese. Back then, Lebanon was under Turkish rule and to escape persecution, many Christians emigrated—to America mainly, but also (sometimes by accident) to Australia.

Callil Betro Fakhry, arriving in 1883, was one of the first Lebanese in Melbourne. With his brother Latoof he set up a business importing 'fancy goods'—things like silk handkerchiefs, ties and hosiery, as well as 'exotic' knick-knacks. These were sold not only at shops in town but by travelling hawkers who sold goods from town to town and farm to farm. Seeing hawkers re-stocking their packs at one of the 'Syrian' warehouses, a journalist likened the scene—'the dark-skinned, black-haired men gathered in groups, amid the gaudy fabrics'—to a brigand's lair from an opera.

Latoof and Callil had their warehouse on Exhibition Street, a few doors from here, and there were plenty of 'fancy repositories' in the neighbourhood. Some of the goods sold were fancier than others. In 1888, John Hanna, a Lebanese dealer with a shop on Exhibition Street, not far from here, got in strife for selling pocket knives containing indecent photographs. It seems that a hole had been drilled in the handle of a cheap knife and a risqué photo inserted, along with a strong magnifying glass. (Top marks for spycraft.) In court, Hanna's lawyer disputed the indecency of the pictures, asking a police witness his views on classical Greek statuary and on the full-length nude that held pride of place in the front bar at Young and Jackson's hotel:*

> *Q. Is the picture of Chloe worse than those photographs in the knives?*
> *A. No, I look upon Chloe as a work of art.*

The case against Hanna was dismissed.

---

* Chloe can still be seen at Young and Jackson's Hotel—corner Flinders and Swanston streets, opposite Flinders Street station.

Arriving in numbers in the 1890s, the Lebanese found themselves caught up in Australia's fixation with whiteness. Their community leaders were at pains to emphasise that they were educated, cultured and Christian. But though they were (however unwillingly) Turkish subjects, and Turkey formed part of Europe, the Lebanese were grouped with migrants from China, India and Afghanistan, branded 'Asiatic' and non-white. After Federation, new migrants from Lebanon weren't welcome and those already here were all but barred from Australian citizenship.

When Australia went to war with Turkey in 1914, Lebanese Australians had to register as 'enemy aliens'. Even so, Callil Fakry's Beirut-born son James managed to enlist in the AIF and—fluent in Arabic and French as well as English—served in Egypt as an interpreter for the 7th Battalion.

Two generations earlier, Abbotomy Michael had witnessed Napoleon III's invasion of Lebanon. The former soldier was a sprightly eighty-four when he settled in Melbourne around 1890, living with his publican son Assid at the Victoria Hotel on this corner. Abbotomy would become a familiar figure around the city, walking miles each day right up until his death at the age of 101.

Next door in Exhibition Street, Shekrey Makbat for years ran a fruit stall with a sly-grog shop behind. In 1925, he'd be implicated in a death of a young woman on his premises.

According to police, Makbat was a 'cocaine fiend' who ran 'snow parties' above his shop, charging attendees two shillings a sniff.

3:N

OLYMPIC THEATRE

CORNER LONSDALE & EXHIBITION STREETS

The first theatre to occupy this corner was the Olympic. Imported in kit form from Manchester in 1855, it was made entirely of galvanised iron and took just six weeks to put up. Sweltering hot in summer, it was nicknamed the Iron Pot. 'The Iron Pot boiled over,' the papers would say after a roaring night at the Olympic. Built to hold 1,500, it could squeeze in hundreds more. They'd be 'clinging to the walls like flies' and even climbing the roof to peep through the ventilators. Between acts, there'd be a rush to the Olympic Hotel next door, whose publican ('so intimate were relations between the drams and the drama') daylighted as the theatre's scenic artist.

Pretty soon though, the Olympic was overshadowed by other, grander theatres, such as the Theatre Royal. 'Irreverent' bats would roost in the Olympic for a few years until it was transformed into Melbourne's first Turkish (or 'Oriental') baths. The audience pit became a swimming pool, thirty metres long and two metres deep, and the bats in the rafters were displaced by plants in hanging baskets. Frigidarium, tepidarium and sudatorium were on the ground floor, and upstairs the old dress circle was arrayed with Turkish rugs and couches, all 'resplendent and showy…in the most approved Eastern fashion'. Female bathers had the place to themselves three afternoons a week.

After a fire in 1866, the empty shell of the Olympic served as furniture warehouse until it was burnt out a second time, by a fire sparked in a storeroom full of dried seaweed, used for stuffing mattresses. In 1894 a hippodrome—a permanent equestrian circus arena—was built on the ruins, echoing the big top of the American Circus, which predated the Iron Pot on this site. (Its proprietor, Fawcett Rowe, had returned to California in 1854 with a fortune.)

3:O

BILKING SQUARE, ROMEO LANE / JULIET TERRACE

56–24 LITTLE BOURKE STREET

A plunge back into Little Bourke Street brings us to a locale that—like Brogans Lane, only more so—is hard to pin down, for all its infamy. Officially, Bilking Square never really existed, yet it was as familiar to Melburnians as any street in Hoddle's grid. Almost daily, it would be name-checked in police reports or lingered over in the slavering slum-tourism screeds that the newspapers loved to run:

> *Turning out of Little Bourke street the explorer of these regions comes upon a barren space giving the idea of a gigantic dust heap…After traversing this open space the pedestrian comes upon a mass of devious rights-of-way in which are innumerable dwellings, mostly diminutive in size and built of wood, and finds upon instituting inquiries that he has reached the haven of Bilking Square.*

The 'square' appeared on no map but filled the space between two rights of way, both now obliterated. Those diminutive dwellings were home, mostly, to prostitutes living in twos and threes, together with their children. Brooding over the cottages stood a mouldering two-storey building of brick and stone, reputedly not just a lair but a *school* for thieves. With three doors and numerous windows—plus the two rights of way—it offered multiple escape routes.

But the main clue to Bilking Square's character was its name. The verb 'bilk' means to cheat and elude, which gives you the bones of it. A typical MO was for a customer, led to a cottage in the square, to pay £1 up front; then, once he was pantsless and recumbent, his companion would duck out to get them both a drink. And that's the last he'd see of her—likewise his wallet which, when he retrieved his trousers, would be missing from the pocket.

Most of the cottages in Bilking Square belonged to Jane Mills, known locally as Big Jane. A fixture in this quarter since the 1850s, she'd done her fair share of bilking and brawling, and it seems likely that she profited not only from the rent but from much of the crime hereabouts. Crossley and Liverpool streets, opposite, were originally Romeo Lane and Juliet Terrace (talk about asking for trouble), and Big Jane owned property in both. She was the proprietress of 'lodging houses'—brothels—which she kept stocked with hopeless, homeless women, whom she supplied with drink and schooled in the art of bilking.

Big Jane's rentals came ready-furnished, notably with sofas that served as stage props for bilkings and untoward deaths. In 1870, Big Jane sold a sofa from one of her houses in Juliet Terrace without noticing that the woman lying on it was dead (from alcoholic poisoning). The body, rolled onto the floor by the buyer, was only discovered next day. That may have been the same house inspected by the back-slums enquiry in 1883, 'an old but substantial-looking' two-storey house with a galvanised-iron 'garret', like a garden shed perched on the roof. Some years before (the story went) this garret had been the scene of a murder, and now was haunted. 'But I take care never to hear the ghost walk,' said the young woman living there, 'for I go to bed drunk every night.'

It was convenient, in a way, to have Big Jane and her cohort penned up together in a few seamy pockets of back-streets Melbourne. The official line ran that 'it is better to let them keep their known haunts than to spread them over the town'. Later, when many city hotels were being considered for closure (see 2:L), the same reasoning would be used to argue for retaining a handful of the seediest pubs: better if 'the unfortunate women' kept their custom to the back streets, 'where their presence would not offend the public'. Nothing, though, could save the likes of the Colonial Family Hotel (on Little Bourke, beyond Juliet Terrace), known locally as 'the dead house'. People *had* been known to meet their death there, it's true, but the term 'dead house' actually referred to a shed in the yard where those too drunk to stagger home could sleep it off.

Lord knows, missionaries had been trying for years to sanitise the vicinity with prayer. A card from the Society for the Promotion of Morality, seen on a Bilking Square mantelpiece, may well have been left by an ancestor of mine who did the rounds of Melbourne's back lanes as a city missionary. For twenty years, he called on 'the fallen and foolish', handing out tracts and saying 'what seemed best'. Brogans Lane he deemed 'a beastly place' and Romeo Lane was 'full of evil and evil only'. Surprisingly, the inhabitants of such 'off-places' often seem to have endured (if not welcomed) his windy lectures about 'their way of life and their duty to themselves, to society and to God'.

George Coppin of the Theatre Royal was instrumental in having the Colonial Family Hotel closed down in 1883, preparatory to building a 'model' lodging house (now Gordon House) directly opposite, with three hundred rooms let at sixpence a night. Coppin won a seat in parliament that same year and must have keenly felt the paradox—if indeed it was one—of such a benighted region existing almost on the doorstep of Parliament House.

3:P

JOB WAREHOUSE
54–62 BOURKE STREET

This row of four shops with upstairs dwellings was built by butcher William Crossley a couple of years before the gold rushes, making them among the oldest Melbourne buildings still standing. Bridging the former Romeo Lane and Juliet Terrace, they ought by rights to be called Friar Laurence's Row, after the cleric who united Shakespeare's star-crossed lovers.

Until 2012, three of the four shops were occupied by Job Warehouse, an overstuffed and eccentric fabric shop opened by the Zeimer brothers, Jacob and Max, in 1950. Doubtless the eccentricity accreted over time, like the window grime, but for as long as I knew of it, Job Warehouse was like something out of a fairytale: a treasure cave-cum-ogre's lair. The Zeimers had no truck with browsers. 'No looking with the hands!' was Max's war cry: it was either buy or get out. Or, ideally, both.

The windows were crammed with rolls of age-stained seersucker and voile and huckaback, pressed tight against the dirty glass. There was something sepulchral about it, like Miss Havisham's parlour. And it was dark in there. I'll admit I was curious, but I never had the guts to venture in.

No, to me, it was Pellegrini's, two doors down, that presented the ultimate test of urban mettle. To order a coffee there, as a young woman, unaccompanied, called for confidence and cleavage, neither of which I had. But still, I'd do it. I'd shoulder through the suit-flannel scrum and catch the eye of the haughty Latin. But then, oh fresh hell, there were those mirror-lined walls…

3:Q

PALACE THEATRE
20 BOURKE STREET

Only the façade of the Palace Theatre remains. The rest came down in 2020, over objections at the loss of yet another live-music venue. The Palace was no architectural gem, but the city council called its demolition 'morally outrageous', arguing that it merited preservation on cultural grounds. Arctic Monkeys had headlined there, for Pete's sake, and

Wilco, Sonic Youth, Queens of the Stone Age, the Killers. And James Brown. In fact, when the Palace was first under threat, there emerged a photo purporting to show Brown's hangdog ghost onstage in the stripped-out theatre. Perhaps it's just how ghosts are, but the spectre in a schlumpy cardigan bore no shade of likeness to the swaggering fireball who, on that same stage in 1988, wore pants so tight they wouldn't zip up.

From this spot, in 1854, you'd have had an uninterrupted view of Melbourne in its entirety: out across the bay from Williamstown to Brighton and inland past the straggling suburbs to the blue smudge of the Dandenongs. Two storeys tall on the Eastern Hill, Mooney's National Hotel boasted the highest elevation in all of Melbourne.

Downstairs was the Chop Cellar. Tom Mooney had advertised for a 'French Yankee Cook' to open an eatery underneath his hotel. What he got was Christopher Pond (younger than when we met him at 3:C): neither Frenchman, Yankee nor cook, but an Englishman, a former printer's apprentice and, at nearly two metres tall, hardly built for cellar-dwelling. The Chop Cellar became the favourite resort of 'fast youth' bent on making a night of it after the theatres closed. (Three doors up was the Salle de Valentino, with Astley's Amphitheatre on the Spring Street corner. 'Theatre' was a polite term for their roster of music-hall and circus acts.) Pond soon moved on and up, to the Café de Paris; but decades later, old Chop Cellar regulars would recollect late-night suppers of stewed tripe, oysters and rump steaks 'reeking from the gridiron' with the misty fondness of Sonic Youth fans revisiting the shell of the Palace Theatre.

Tom Mooney, before he was publican of the National Hotel, had been a journalist in Dublin. In gold-rush Melbourne, he'd take a leading part in the movement to 'unlock the lands' from the squatters' grip and win gold diggers and working men the right to vote—universal suffrage, so-called. The People's League met weekly at Mooney's hotel and in 1855 he stood (unsuccessfully) for parliament on a platform of 'a Farm, a Vote and a Rifle' for every man.

High up under the roof of the National Hotel were servants' quarters, hardly more than crawl-spaces. Legend says that Mooney's countryman Peter Lalor laid low there for months after the 'scrummage' at Eureka Stockade in 1854 left him a one-armed fugitive. But if Lalor was grateful for the bolt-hole, I'll bet he could have done without the racket from the Athenaeum Assembly Rooms behind the hotel. Open nightly from nine until four, the dancehall was nowhere near as genteel as its name suggests. Melbourne's mayor called it 'one of the greatest abominations in the city' and the National Hotel was threatened with closure unless the doorway between it and the Athenaeum was bricked up—along with another doorway leading to another riotous pick-up joint: the euphoniously suggestive Tuck & Beddings, pastrycooks and confectioners, next door.

In fact, Mooney's hotel and its satellites would be 'specially alluded to' in a complaint drawing parliament's attention to the 'disorderly, immoral and scandalous conduct in the public streets, consequent upon the laxity of the police authorities, in reference to prostitutes'. (Yikes, they were leaking out of the back streets.) The solution was obvious: the hotel's name was changed to the Excelsior and, lo, it was soon extolled as 'one of the finest in the City of Melbourne', frequented by 'persons having to attend the Parliament House'. Not that *that* was any guarantee of probity. Rumours still abound of tunnels leading from beneath Parliament House to the east end's choicest bordellos—for all we know, grazing the Chop Cellar along the way.

'Melbourne Landmarks Disappearing—Another One Doomed' was the headline in 1911, when the old Excelsior Hotel was about to be 'cleared away' to make room for the 3,000-seat National Amphitheatre. The new name for the kind of acts once staged at Astley's and the Salle de Valentino was *vaudeville*—'the amusement-octopus of the twentieth century'—and that's what pulled crowds at the Amphitheatre. At least it did for a few years, until moving pictures slayed the octopus. Then the Amphitheatre became a picture theatre, the Palace. Over the next forty years, it would be successively renamed the New Palace, the Apollo and the St James. The old theatre had been dormant for years when it was reborn, in 1987, as the Metro nightclub.

Pop icon Ian 'Molly' Meldrum hosted the star-studded opening night, broadcast live on the former Channel 0. With a giant disco ball splintering light from Art Deco chandeliers above the dance floor, the Metro was hailed as 'the most beautiful club ever'. Olivia Newton-John, beamed in from LA, vowed she'd be 'boogying' there next time she came to town. Rick Astley on vinyl was one thing, but it would be as a live-music venue that the Metro made its name over the next twenty-plus years. Somehow though, it would end its days as the Palace.

Awaiting demolition, the old Palace surrendered some of its secrets: a room above the upper balcony filled with jumbled furniture and old newspapers; and, behind the cloakroom wall, a 1980s-era time capsule yielding an eloquent assemblage of tram ticket and empty condom packet. But when the big diggers moved in and the Deep Excavation signs went up on the hoardings, it was the cellar I wondered about. Did they uncover chop bones and oyster shells? Or a tunnel, perhaps?

3:R

LE MONDE CAFÉ
12 BOURKE STREET

Hard to believe there was a time within living memory (COVID lockdowns excepted) when it wasn't easy to find a cup of coffee in Melbourne on a Sunday. Until 1996, archaic weekend trading laws meant that shops couldn't sell a hammer or a toaster on Sunday—unless they masqueraded as booksellers. Smart-aleck traders would test the laws by offering, say, a free billiard table with every book purchased. The upshot was that the city on Sundays was pretty much a wasteland—rattling trams, but not much else. Offering relief to the famished suburban soul in this vicinity were the Paperback Bookshop, sandwiched between Job Warehouse and Pellegrini's, and the Whole Earth Bookshop opposite. (Neither sold billiard tables.)

Pellegrini's was always open, but—the noise, those mirrors—it was never the best place for propping with a book. Luckily, there was Le Monde, on this spot. Serious young socialists, shy guys in slacks and glasses, used to congregate here to play chess and murmur (not shout) about revolution. The café's entranceway was laid in mosaic, with *Le Monde* picked out, black on white, in spiky, vaguely Soviet-style lettering. Inside, the lighting was dim and there was a tamped-down feel to Le Monde. Guy Rundle, writing years later in the *Age*, said the Romanian couple who ran the place had been 'engaged in an argument that seemed to have begun at about the time of World War II'.

3:S

PARLIAMENT HOUSE

The design for Parliament House was drawn up in 1855, but its construction would take thirty-five years. It was built in stages: the two parliamentary chambers, the library, Queen's Hall, the imposing colonnade and the stairs. Cost was the main reason for eking out construction, but there was also the matter of building stone.

A lack of quality local stone posed a problem for Melbourne's builders from the start. (See 6:G.) True, there was plenty of bluestone (basalt) to be had, but it was seen as too gloomy to be suitable for public buildings. Sandstone like Sydney's—fine-grained, white and hard-wearing—was what was wanted, but even a government-sponsored competition failed to find any local sandstone that looked good and aged well. Stone from a quarry on the south side of the Yarra was coarse-grained and turned 'rusty' with age.

For a while, Bacchus Marsh sandstone seemed promising but, used in the façade of a bank in Elizabeth Street, showed 'strong symptoms of decay after a very brief exposure to the atmosphere'. And the Customs House (see 2:H) was 'crumbling away like a delicate piece of pastry' while still under construction.

Building stone was imported from Tasmania, from New Zealand and, with gritted teeth, from Sydney. It even looked for a while as if the completion of Parliament House, its grand public face, would rely on New South Wales stone. Just in time, a source of sandstone fit for the task was discovered at Heatherlie in the Grampians. So irate was one member of parliament at the prospect of Sydney sandstone being chosen instead that he had a pillar of Heatherlie stone mounted near the Exhibition Buildings 'to express his indignation' (as it says on the plaque) 'and to show the enduring qualities of local stone'.

While building the first stage of Parliament House, stonemasons downed tools in demand of a shorter working day. Ten hours, six days a week was the norm. But the hot Australian sun made long work days even longer. Besides, workers—gold-rush immigrants, most of them—wanted time for other things: not just recreation and rest, but education and self-improvement. 'We have come 16,000 miles to better our condition,' said James Galloway of the stonemasons' union, 'and not to act the mere part of machinery.' The eight-hour working day won by Melbourne stonemasons in 1856 was a nineteenth-century landmark every bit as prominent as Parliament House.

When Victoria's newly bicameral (two-house) parliament first sat in 1856, a top hat formed part of every parliamentarian's outfit. Early on, Charles Gavan Duffy MLA caused a stir by not doffing his hat when rising to address the Speaker. An ex-member of British Parliament, Duffy assured his Victorian colleagues that hat-on was correct protocol, after which members were 'recognised' by the Speaker only if wearing a hat. The rest of the time their headgear lay piled on the table in the middle of the chamber, making the scramble to grab a hat and catch the Speaker's attention look like an after-dinner parlour game.

Finally completed in 1889, the Parliament House façade incorporates a feature hidden from the casual sightseer. High up on either side of the entrance are narrow horizontal slits that give a clear line of sight down Bourke Street. The 1890s were a time of unrest, with mass unemployment, strikes—even talk of revolution. In the event of strife outside parliament, marksmen would be able to fire on a mob through the slits in the front wall. As far as anyone knows, though, the embrasures have never been used other than for ventilation. In fact, that may well have been their intended purpose. Flanking the grand colonnade are internal stairwells, on each landing of which originally stood...a toilet cubicle. The position of these conveniences is said to have coincided exactly with the chamfered 'gun-slits'.

3:T

DWIGHT'S BOOKSHOP
13 BOURKE STREET

Here, in the 1860s, H. T. Dwight kept Melbourne's best second-hand bookshop, a meeting-place for the city's bohemian literati.

The croaky-voiced Dwight imported old books by the hundredweight. He acquired stock locally, too, from the liquidated colonial libraries of well-read Melburnians returning 'home' once the heat went out of the gold rushes. In 1869, Dwight had for sale a heap of books that had belonged to R. H. Horne—poet, friend to Pre-Raphaelites and contributor to Dickens' *Household Words*—who'd just ended his colonial sojourn. In the 'fourpenny box' on the footpath a journalist from the *Age* spied a copy of Robert Browning's *Pauline*, inscribed by the author to his friend Horne. But when he returned in his lunch hour with fourpence, the book was gone—and he kicked himself ever after.

R. H. Horne's epic poem *Orion* had been a literary sensation of the 1840s. But though it ran to ten editions, it hadn't made him rich. In 1852 he joined the rush to Victoria where top-notch testimonials landed him a string of positions, as commander of the gold escort, mining registrar and commissioner of the Yan Yean water supply. In his spare time, Horne was a vigneron, playwright, stunt-swimmer and social pariah—he never went anywhere without his guitar.

3:U

DR L. L. SMITH / SALVATION ARMY LIMELIGHT BRIGADE

69 BOURKE STREET

Here stood 'the beautiful Cosmophenopolygraphicon', or Dr Louis L. Smith's Royal Polytechnic Institute and Anatomical Museum. The son of an influential London theatrical figure, Smith was as much showman as he was medico. He boasted of spending £3,000 a year on newspaper advertisements that traded on men's fears about the consequences of 'early indiscretions'—i.e. masturbation and venereal disease—and women's of unwanted pregnancy. Those reluctant to confide in their own doctor were encouraged to 'throw off all false modesty and apply for help before it is too late' by consulting Dr Smith via the post (fee £1, payable in advance).

In 1862, he added to his consulting rooms and private hospital a polytechnic institute modelled on a London enterprise of the same name, bringing 'rational amusement' to Melbourne's theatrical quarter—a blend of education, entertainment and hucksterism. There were lectures illustrated with 'dissolving views' (lantern slides) and 'brilliant' experiments demonstrating 'the Wonders of Chemistry'. Also, every Monday and Saturday, laughing gas. To balance the instruction, there was 'appropriate music', often in the shape of balladry, and every evening at nine, Dr Smith himself lectured on sexual health in the Anatomical Museum.

The museum, originally open to all who paid the polytechnic's one-shilling admission fee, included waxen anatomical cutaways of the digestive and reproductive systems. Public objections to their 'graphic' nature forced Smith to separate the museum and limit entry to men only. Women were, however, the main focus of his in-person medical practice and private hospital, where Smith specialised in 'the diseases of married life, nervous affections and debility, midwifery, and the diseases of women'. (His speciality wasn't just professional: twice-married, he fathered fourteen children.) In 1858, he was charged with procuring an abortion and, though acquitted, never quite shook off the stigma.

L. L. Smith lived life large. With his waxed mustachios, diamond ring and boisterous wit, he was at home among the bohemian crowd at Dwight's bookshop. But while doctoring-by-mail and his cure-all Vegetable Pills ('For Biliousness, Sick Headache...') made him a rich man, they didn't win him respectability. Even as a member of parliament, he was more scorned than respected. Once, in the House, a fellow MP scoffed that any motion proposed by Smith 'would be reduced to the level of a quack advertisement'. Smith, who must have been hard of hearing, thought he'd been called 'a quack and a courtesan'. He duly biffed his antagonist in the parliamentary luncheon-room and was escorted to a cell in the dungeon to cool off.

Smith's Royal Polytechnic failed as a profit-turning educational institution and for decades would be just another hall hosting travelling stage acts, boxing matches and meetings of the Free Thought Society. In 1894 the building became the Salvation Army's Melbourne headquarters, with an attic room adapted as a photographic studio for the Limelight Brigade. The Salvation Army had been in the 'limelight' (magic lantern) business since 1891, producing narrative slideshows of holiday spots, biblical scenes and even the slums of Little Bourke Street. For eighteen years, the Limelight Brigade (later Department) would be at the cutting edge of cinematic development, making some of Australia's earliest moving pictures and presenting spectacular shows that combined short films, lantern slides, gramophone soundtracks and live music.

During the first decade of the twentieth century—that is, the first decade of cinema—nearly eighty per cent of Australian-made films originated upstairs at 69 Bourke Street.

The Limelight Department was known internationally as an innovator in moving-picture production. In 1900, more than two thousand Melburnians filled the town hall for the premiere of *Soldiers of the Cross*, a movie/lantern-slide hybrid that has since been hailed as the world's first feature film. The Salvation Army toured its limelight productions to towns and cities all over Australia and New Zealand, making converts to cinema and Salvationism.

Then, in 1909, the Salvation Army's new Australasian commander shut down the Limelight Department, calling it 'incompatible with true Salvationism'. Equipment was sold off, film footage destroyed and the attic studio abandoned. Over time, building alterations would seal off the studio, making it a time capsule. Only in 2011 was the disinterred Limelight Department opened to visitors.

3:V

EASTERN MARKET / SOUTHERN CROSS HOTEL

CORNER BOURKE & EXHIBITION STREETS

Here, starting in the 1840s, was the Eastern Market. It was the city's main outlet for fresh produce for thirty years, until the Queen Victoria Market took over. What lived on and lingered longest in memory, though, was the Paddy's Market staged here on Saturday nights: the open-air showground of Melbourne's theatre district.

The whole of working Melbourne would flock to Paddy's Market to blow some pennies and blow off some steam. There were sideshows and fortune-tellers, hucksters, brass bands, preachers, shooting galleries, tooth-pullers, oyster stalls, and no end of cheap trifles to be had. You could have seen (and heard) it from space.

In the super-heated decade or so following the discovery of gold, when Victoria was hailed as 'a laboratory of democracy', the Eastern Market was the closest thing Melbourne had to a public square. It was also pretty close to Parliament House, which lent a glint of insurrection to open-air meetings held among the shuttered market stalls. Just a block downhill from parliament, protests over 'the land question'—the long struggle to wrest public lands from the squatter fraternity that dominated the all-powerful Upper House—boiled up and, in 1860, boiled over into a riot. Protesters stormed the doors of Parliament House, smashing windows and jostling parliamentarians. Legislation was hastily passed 'for securing the freedom of the deliberations of Parliament and for preventing disorderly meetings'—essentially, outlawing open-air assemblies in the environs of Parliament House while either house was sitting. Later that decade, the anonymous author of *Democratic Government in Victoria* would assert—ironically, but with a touch of pride—that 'a Melbourne mob is vastly superior to any mob which can be seen in Europe'.

The Eastern Market hollowed out in the years after Federation. The phrenologists, herbalists and masseurs put down roots in the dingy passageways of the Eastern Arcade alongside, while the market itself degenerated to a 'dreary morgue...a vast, rambling monstrosity', increasingly disreputable and off-limits. Only after the 1956 Olympics, when the city's old-style hostelries—with their threadbare carpets and bathrooms down the hall—were found wanting, did Melbourne finally embrace the twentieth century. The 'anachronism' of the Eastern Market would yield its site to a fourteen-storey international hotel built by Pan American Airways.

The Southern Cross would, in its turn, become passé and give way to the towers that stand here now. But in its heyday, it was the last word in Melbourne high-life, hosting the important awards ceremonies—TV's Logies, football's Brownlow Medal—and election-night functions for the Liberal Party. In 1964, when the Beatles stayed there, the hotel loomed over scenes more clamorous and insurgent than anything the old Eastern Market had witnessed: Bourke Street East bunged tight, volatile with hairspray fumes and thousands of girls, ululating. The Southern Cross held the distinction of having billeted *five* Beatles: the fifth was the drummer who filled in while Ringo was having his tonsils out. Afterwards, brass plaques would memorialise the Beatles' rooms; but as far as anyone remembers, there never was a Jimmie Nicol Suite.

WALK 4
I WILL SEE YOU THERE

In which we consider morality, headgear, justice, Armageddon and the parts of an ox

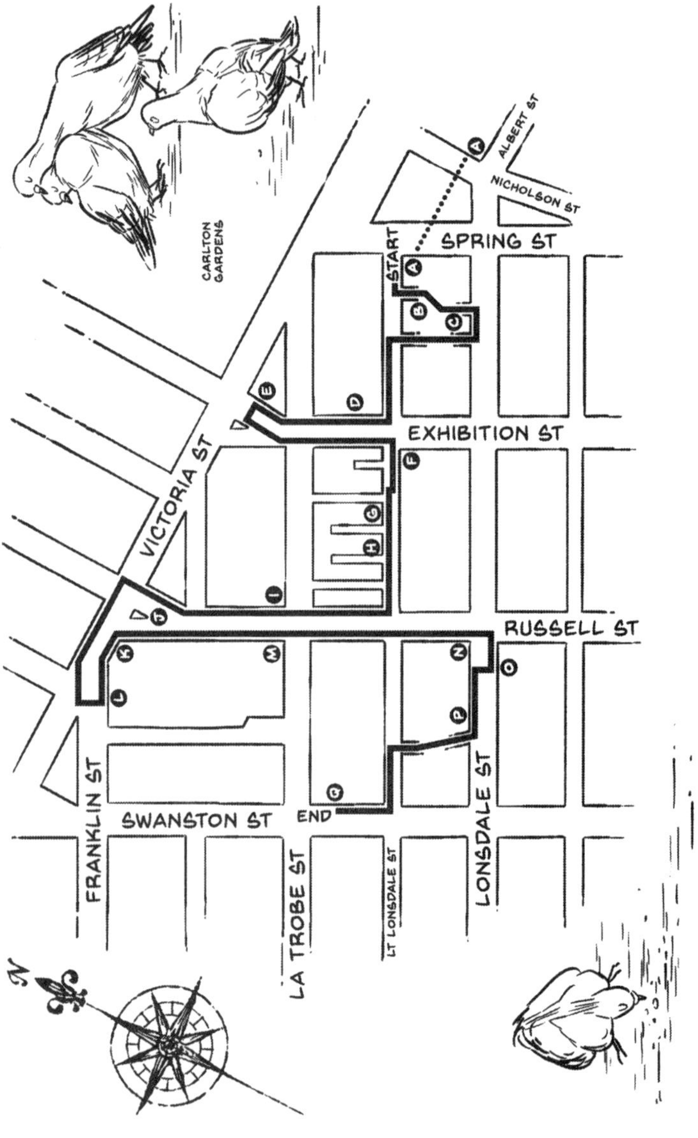

CARLTON GARDENS
ALBERT ST
NICHOLSON ST
SPRING ST
START
EXHIBITION ST
VICTORIA ST
RUSSELL ST
LONSDALE ST
SWANSTON ST
END
FRANKLIN ST
LA TROBE ST
LT LONSDALE ST
N

ICI (ORICA) HOUSE

SEEN FROM CORNER SPRING & LITTLE LONSDALE STREETS

Remember the Australian Building, down in the ditch of Elizabeth Street? For nearly seventy years it set Melbourne's height limit—until 1958, when ICI House raised the roof.

Back then, cool cats called it a 'cloud-kisser'. The city council, which had for so long kept a lid on the city, made a show of reluctance when it first saw plans for the grey grid tower. But really, post-Olympics, Melbourne was ready to get high. The council gave the go-ahead for ICI House, then feigned astonishment that they'd approved a building 230 feet high—almost a hundred feet taller than the long-standing height-limit. The plans, as made public, had proposed a height of *203* feet but 'thanks to a town hall typist's error' (that old ruse!) the digits got scrambled, and…oh, well.

It took fifteen tonnes of putty to fix in place the panes of Belgian glass that gave ICI House its cool-as-an-icecube look. The architects had claimed there would be 'light and ventilation and outlook from four sides', but in fact the narrow east and west walls were solid concrete, with glass overlaid to give the *impression* of windows. Not long after it was finished, the building's west wall began shedding panes of glass as the putty was seared by the afternoon sun. Rectifying the problem took years: Melburnians with long memories still think of ICI House as 'the deciduous building'.

At the opening of ICI House, dignitaries attending the ceremony on the top floor were treated to a bird's-eye view of a public urinal in Nicholson Street below. The *pissoir*, one of the city's wrought-iron treasures, was given a roof soon after.

As a kid, I loved ICI House: tallest building in Melbourne *and* my dad worked there. He was in marketing for a paint firm, an ICI subsidiary. (We got to name some of the car duco colours: *Purgatory Purple* was one of Mum's, and my brother came up with *Yuk*, the baby-poo brown of a zillion '70s-era Volkswagens.) I'm pretty sure I never set foot inside ICI House, but a promotional film made at the time of its opening showed a sleek and shiny fit-out based on ICI products like perspex and vinyl. And on every flat surface: an ash tray. Which was convenient for Dad. Had he not been free to smoke at his desk he'd have got through only one pack of ciggies a day instead of three, and would have taken far longer to smoke himself to death.

LITTLE LON
17 CASSELDEN PLACE

Here was Little Lon, or part of it. One of the city's most derided slum-quarters for fifty years or more, Little Lon extended from Lonsdale Street to La Trobe and Exhibition to Spring, with Little Lonsdale Street as its spine. Pretty much *all* the laneways hereabouts shared the same unsavoury reputation as their Little Bourke counterparts.

Little Lon was crime-ridden, the pubs were blood-houses. City missionaries like St Mary McKillop made a special project of Little Lon, seeking to 'reclaim' poor women from sex work and to educate their children.

Successive attempts at slum clearance saw the area become less residential, more industrial, home to countless cabinetmakers' workshops and factories making everything from steam boilers to ice cream. But still, there were cottages crowded together in the back lanes—like this one, the only survivor of a row of six built in the 1870s. Most Little Lon dwellings weren't of brick but timber, and of the improvised, ramshackle kind we've already seen condemned by the back-slums enquiry of 1883.

Light has been shone anew on Little Lon since the 1980s, when heritage regulations first mandated archaeological investigations as a prerequisite of building projects in the

CBD. Several bouts of excavation have lifted and sifted through the traces of lives lived here. And in the process, Little Lon has found itself ennobled.

Where once they were compared to 'brute beasts in the mire', the women, immigrants and outcasts who peopled this neighbourhood have been recast as gritty survivors: brought low, perhaps, but possessing dignity and a glint of self-determination. The archaeological finds suggest they were also in possession of modest treasures, relics of past lives or else signs of aspiration. Among the Little Lon artefacts at Melbourne Museum—besides the commonplace tobacco pipes and sewer pipes, bottles and toys, coins and crockery fragments—are items of fine-quality china and jewellery. Thus have the former residents of Little Lon been retroactively dignified as strivers, not all that different from us.

Paradoxical, isn't it, that it took the obliteration of Little Lon to bring the place and its inhabitants back into view? Of the fourteen named lanes (not counting the never-named courts and yards and curlicued 'back places'), all but four have been built over. Yet Melburnians are more aware than ever of Little Lon, an inner-city neighbourhood where even those who wallowed kept one eye on the stars.

Speaking of stars, I first saw the Southern Cross (the constellation, not the hotel) on the 1988 Little Lon archaeological dig. After a day's digging, we'd sit around a bonfire and drink beer, refilling with our bottles a hole we'd earlier emptied of long-dead marines. I was reclining, bone-tired, in a tilted-up wheelbarrow when someone pointed out the Southern Cross directly above us. 'Huh,' I remember thinking, 'it's been there all this time and I didn't know.' Same with Little Lon.

BROTHELDOM / THE MISSING MACE

MADAME BRUSSELS LANE → LONSDALE STREET

With the wholesale redevelopment of the Little Lon block since 1988, Casselden Place (originally a dead end), along with Gorman Alley (ditto), have found themselves tributaries to a meandering new through-way to Lonsdale Street, Madame Brussels Lane.

Madame Brussels (real name: Caroline Hodgson, later Pohl) ran a high-class brothel, Bellevue-villa, on Lonsdale Street, at the exact spot where her eponymous lane now debouches. Over the course of thirty years, starting in the 1870s, Madame B acquired wealth and notoriety in equal measure. In 1906, the scandal-mongering *Truth* newspaper claimed the scalp of Sir Samuel Gillott, a government minister and former lord mayor, when it exposed him as Madame B's long-time financier. Juiced up on alliteration pills, the *Truth*'s editor trashed her as a 'hellish harridan' and a 'feculent fiend in female form', and wrote of the 'blind alley...by which her crapulous, concupiscent clients may enter and leave her lair of lechery practically unobserved'. He meant Gorman Alley, which ended at Madame B's back fence.

Just a few doors along Lonsdale Street from Madame Brussels' was the likewise notorious Boccaccio House, run by Annie Wilson. On paper a humble boarding-house keeper, Wilson stabled three ponies and a gig, owned shares in the colony's leading goldmines and had several magistrates on a string. She served champagne and whisky at all hours, yet was never asked to show her liquor licence (just as well: she didn't have one). And around 1890, Boccaccio House got a phone line connected, allegedly so that members of parliament could be recalled to the chamber in the event of a division.

Some time between midnight and lunchtime one Friday in October 1891, a lock was forced on a case in the Speaker's room at Parliament House, and the ceremonial mace disappeared.

Following the tradition of Britain's House of Commons, no business can proceed in Victoria's lower house unless the mace rests in place at the centre of the chamber. The missing mace was about 1.5 metres long and made of gold-plated silver. Suspicion fell first on a handyman seen leaving for lunch with a long, skinny brown-paper parcel. (Remember, this was pre-baguette Melbourne.) Police searched his home to no avail, and the trail went cold—at least, it *seemed* to. A year later, there was still no trace of the missing mace. But rumours had begun to surface...

Parliamentarians were especially on the nose just then. In the slump that ended Victoria's boom, countless dodgy political dealings had come to light. Now the newspapers carried tales—said to be common knowledge among MPs and the police—of a midnight spree in the Legislative Assembly chamber, following which:

> *one of Annie Wilson's boarders, with several other sirens, invaded the Speaker's rooms and, in a spirit of devilment, marched to the Lonsdale Street house, carrying off the Mace as a trophy.*

At Boccaccio House, the story went, a mock parliament was held, with the mace playing who-knew-what profane part. (It unscrewed into ten pieces, so...plenty of options.) An official enquiry quizzed Annie Wilson and dozens more witnesses, but came up empty-handed.

When Wilson moved her operations to Perth in 1895, Melburnians wondered if the mace had gone with her. Boccaccio House would be replaced by factories some time before World War I, along with Madame Brussels' Bellevue-villa. Decades later, when archaeologists began digging up Little Lon, every second bystander had the same question: *Did you find the mace yet?* No such luck. Also unfound were the tunnels claimed by urban legend to have linked the Parliament House and the Lonsdale Street brothels. (How else had the mace made such a clean getaway?) But popular interest in the fate of the mace revived to such an extent that a reward was offered for information leading to its recovery. The fifty thousand dollars is still unclaimed.

A little way downhill, archaeologists excavating a backyard cesspit found a deep stash of liquor bottles a cut above the usual beer and gin. There were bottles that had held champagne and fine wines (some were branded Chateau Margaux), as well as empties left by 'the green fairy' (absinthe), all intermingled with oyster shells by the hundreds. The cesspit's contents dated to the 1860s and '70s, when the backyard had belonged to Alicia Bond's grocery shop at 60 Lonsdale Street. Turns out Mrs Bond had earlier kept a brothel in nearby Stephen (Exhibition) Street—'one of the most disorderly in that part of town', which was saying something. Married to a wastrel, then as a widow, she'd supported her children by taking in washing before turning to sex work. On the evidence of her rubbish pit, Mrs Bond's Lonsdale Street establishment—the presumed brothel for which her shop was a front—must have attracted its fair share of 'rich and influential scallywags'. Yet somehow it avoided notice, or at least exposure, by police and the press.

Right at the bottom of a cesspit not far from Mrs Bond's, beneath a thousand or more carefully stacked bottles, archaeologists found what had once been a white cotton shirt, now mud-brown and rotten, wrapped around a mass of bottle corks. There were 1,198—I know, because I was given the job of counting and sorting them by type. The thinking was that the empties had been 'put in storage' with a view to shortly refilling them with hooch. Corks were expensive to buy new, so used ones had been laid away to re-stopper the bottles. Now, exposed to the air after more than a hundred years, they quickly turned mouldy and had to be reburied—along with my putative expertise.

Madame Brussels Lane was created when the thirty-four-storey Urban Workshop (who are they kidding?) was planted on Little Lon's middle portion. The developers claimed that their building 'responds' to the pattern of laneways it displaced. A sample of Little Lon artefacts is on display in the foyer and in a courtyard off Madame B's Lane there's the stump of a river redgum: a rare relic of Melbourne-before-Melbourne.

4:D

ANTONIO PERUGIA'S STUDIO

308 EXHIBITION STREET

Here stood the studio of Florentine-born modeller and sculptor Antonio Perugia. As well as shaping clay or wax prototypes for other sculptors to recast in more durable stuff, Perugia produced his own work in the statuary line. Classic-style statues cast from plaster or cement were his mainstay. For churches he did saints (St Joseph was a specialty), while subjects like Venus with Mirror, Pandora and Psyche or Bacchus and the Three Graces were just the thing for public parks. One of Perugia's first commissions was to supply statues for the Fitzroy Gardens.

He also tried his hand at waxworks. A waxworks exhibition that opened in Bourke Street in 1857 would still be running sixty years later, long outlasting the freak shows, anatomical museums and wild animal menageries that had vied for the sensation-seeking crowd mid-century. In an age before there were even illustrated newspapers—let alone newsreels or TV—waxworks were as close as you got to lifelike images of celebrities.

For a travelling show in 1862, Perugia fashioned wax effigies of Abraham Lincoln and Jefferson Davis, Garibaldi, the Prince of Wales, John Pascoe Fawkner, bushrangers Dan Morgan and Frank Gardiner, Mrs Scott ('the Mansfield murderess'), a bearded lady and the Extraordinary Fat Girl from Sydney. But the star exhibit comprised wax tableaux of tragical scenes from the Burke and Wills expedition. There was 'The Return to Cooper's Creek' ('so close has the artist approached to nature that the visitor becomes deeply interested in the fate of these great explorers'), 'The Death of Wills' ('painful yet pleasing to look upon') and 'Burke Expiring in the Arms of King!' ('the gem of the Exhibition'). Their creator, Antonio Perugia, was billed as 'the first sculptor in the southern hemisphere'—meaning not literally the *first* but the *best*.

Running a business in a neighbourhood like Little Lon can't have been easy. Perugia had his share of run-ins with drunks, larrikins and thieves, including an old woman who hid a bust of Shakespeare under her shawl. His own wife, Mary, was inclined to go 'on the beer' for weeks at a time, sometimes 'turning her children out of doors at night'. When Perugia shot himself in his studio in 1895, the headline told the story: 'Despair and Death. Totally Blind. Domestic Troubles.' Carried on by his son (also Antonio), the studio of Perugia and Son would specialise in plaster models for art schools and, for the Mines Department, replica gold nuggets.

4:E

ROYAL SOCIETY OF VICTORIA

EXHIBITION STREET, NEAR VICTORIA PARADE

Looking like a primordial jellybean on stilts is the Royal Society of Victoria's centenary monument (1859–1959). In fact, it's a smooth-worn granite boulder, a 'glacial erratic' brought from Antarctica and charmingly mounted on three legs *to commemorate the completion of one hundred years of endeavour by this Society in its work for the advancement of science.* That hundred years' endeavour began with the doomed Victorian Exploring Expedition, led by Burke and Wills.

In August 1860, two days before the exploring party set off to cross the continent south to north (and back again), its members assembled here, at Royal Society HQ, to get their marching orders. Sir William Stawell, expedition committee chairman, exhorted them to speak up if they had any misgivings about the undertaking ahead. 'It is not yet too late,' he assured them, as if they were flighty grooms:

> *Any man who has that lurking feeling in his heart had much better say so now, or, if not, for ever after hold your peace.*

No one made a peep. The expedition's success, Stawell went on, would depend on their 'most absolute obedience' to Robert O'Hara Burke, a country policeman seemingly ill-equipped for the role of expedition leader. Burke, in response, praised the camels and declared, 'I will not go forward for fear of being called a coward, nor remain behind to be called a fool.' Avoidance of mockery hardly counts as a noble motivation. Still, he added, 'If I do not succeed, there will be a good reason for it.'

Burke would die on the journey, as would his sidekick William Wills and five more expeditioners. Also twelve Indigenous people, massacred by a party sent in search of the missing heroes. And all for no good reason.

4:F

CITY FREE KINDERGARTEN

CORNER LITTLE LONSDALE & EXHIBITION STREETS

Built in 1859 as the Mickveh Yisrael synagogue and Hebrew school, this building would later house an outpost of the Salvation Army ministering to the inhabitants of Little Lon. In 1910, the first free kindergarten in the CBD opened here. The kindergarten movement was still fairly new and had been run up till then on a charitable basis. The government contributed to the City Free Kindergarten in the hope that its influence would eventually 'solve the problem of the Melbourne slums':

> *Its object is to take hold of the child till he or she reaches school age, and to supplant the lessons of the slum and the gutter by simple instruction in goodness, in civilisation…*

To Dr William Maloney, Labor MP for Melbourne, a free kindergarten was the least the government owed the city's poor. Maloney campaigned for a maternity allowance and birth control and, as early as 1889, had introduced a women's suffrage bill in parliament. (That bill was the first of its kind in the British Empire. It failed to pass, as would *seventeen* subsequent bills before Victorian women—the last in Australia—finally won the right to vote in state elections.) 'A destitute woman,' said Maloney at the opening of the City Free Kindergarten, 'should be able to go to the Government and say, *My child lacks clothes and food, and it is your duty to save this future unit of Australia.*' Stirring socialistic stuff.

4:G

MRS HOLDSWORTH, STRAW-BONNET CLEANER

EXPLORATION LANE

Curiously, given the florid displays of public mourning that followed the deaths of Burke and Wills, Exploration Lane is the nearest thing to a street named in their honour within the city grid.* And even then it was a second-hand homage: the lane got its name from the Exploration Hotel, which had been named for the doomed expedition. Evidently the Wesley (Methodist) Church exerted no sobering sway over its neighbourhood, since the Exploration was one of four hotels between here and Russell Street.

Before the exploration or its namesakes, a Mrs Holdsworth lived on this same spot, cleaning straw bonnets for a living. You might think a soft sponge and stiff brush would do

* There's a Wills Street just north of La Trobe. Bourke Street (with an o) was named for Sir Richard Bourke, who was Governor of New South Wales when Hoddle drew the Melbourne grid.

the trick, but straw-bonnet cleaning was a rare art that combined elements of bomb-making and alchemy. And it took *days*. First, white clay was applied, then salt of sorrel, then a weak solution of pearl ash in water, followed by a good soaping, after which the bonnet was hung in the sun to dry. ('The bonnet must on no account be hung out if the weather is damp,' warned an 1850 manual of domestic economy, 'and it must be brought in before sunset.') After cleaning came whitening, for which the bonnet was—counterintuitively—hung over a dish of burning charcoal strewn with powdered brimstone (sulphur) in a tightly sealed room or cupboard. After seven hours, the door could be opened and the bonnet retrieved—'as soon as you find you can do so without inconvenience from the fumes'—and hung outside until the rotten-egg smell had left it. Next came the stiffening: shavings of buffalo-hide vellum were boiled to form a thick jelly in which the bonnet was twice coated, each time followed by a wash and dry. Finally it was placed on a bonnet-block and ironed, 'exerting all your strength'. That was the straw headpiece done. Before the bonnet could be called properly cleaned, its lining and trim required separate refurbishment, to the same exhaustive extent. For her trouble, Mrs Holdsworth might be paid one shilling and threepence—roughly a third of a labourer's weekly wage.

4:H

WOODEN TELEGRAPH POLE

BENNETTS LANE

Lay your hand on power pole no. 75843, one of the few bare wooden poles left in the CBD. (Its neighbour, 85676, is braced in metal to head height.) This is a descendant of the many-branched telegraph poles that formed a linear forest down one side of every Melbourne street for long enough that 'telegraph pole' became the generic name for any post holding wires aloft. By the time Frank Wilmot wrote his modernist ode 'To a Telegraph Pole' in the late 1920s, the poles carried mostly telephone lines and, in the CBD, even those were being routed underground. Back then, telegraph poles were painted white, the better to see and skirt them in the comparatively unlit city at night.

Wilmot's pen-name, Furnley Maurice, spliced *Fern*tree Gully and Beau*maris*, the mountain and coastal limits of his hometown. In 'To a Telegraph Pole' he evoked a Melbourne that's still recognisable almost a hundred years on (*The lanes are full of young men swallowing beer…The swelling and failing moan of the street trams…*), as backdrop to a hardwood encounter linking a laneway like this one with the mountain-ash forests east of the city:

I saw you in your slender whiteness there;
I put my hand upon your painted side;
You quivered in a sudden mountain air
And I was back to where your friends abide.
The brown ferns sway,
And your long rustling fingers of soft green
Plash in the light and give the light away...

4:1

POLICE HEADQUARTERS
336 RUSSELL STREET

The blond-brick façade of the old Russell Street police headquarters was familiar to TV viewers all over Australia in the 1960s and '70s, as backdrop to the opening credits of the pioneering cop show *Homicide*. An early model Falcon would execute a U-turn to the kerb and unpack Jack Fagen, Leonard Teale, Norman Yemm and their fedora'd brethren. The clench-jawed Teale in particular had authority stamped all over him, never more so than when issuing his trademark command, 'Take it down to Forensics, Pete.' Pete was never seen, except as a hand and Pelaco-shirt-clad forearm obtruding from off-screen right to take custody of an evidence bag.

When spunky young George Mallaby joined the cast of *Homicide* in 1967, he was sent to buy himself a hat.

Being of the post-JFK generation, he contrived to avoid having to wear a hat on the show by buying the most ludicrous one he could find. But the wardrobe mistress loved it, and so Mallaby was stuck for the duration with a ridiculous pork pie a couple of sizes too small for his head. Add lederhosen and he'd have passed for one of the Von Trapp Family Singers.

Mallaby, hatless, would later appear in *The Box* as an adulterous TV executive and habitué of the Chateau Commodore Hotel in Lonsdale Street. (See 3:K.) Joe Cocker, arrested shirtless and shoeless at the same hostelry, spent a night in the cells here at police HQ.

4:J

EIGHT-HOURS MONUMENT

TRAFFIC ISLAND, CORNER RUSSELL & VICTORIA STREETS

As a plain pedestal, this monument used to stand in Spring Street, not far from Parliament House. It was relocated here, close to Trades Hall, and completed in 1903. The crowning insignia of three 8s within a circle represents a worker's day divided into three equal parts: work, recreation and rest.

From 1879, Eight-Hour Day (later Labour Day) was commemorated with an annual public holiday and a procession through Melbourne's streets of workers carrying banners denoting their trade guilds and unions. By the 1950s, Labour Day had pretty much lost its point, with the union movement preferring to parade on May Day. A pageant of flower-themed floats along Swanston Street during the royal visit in 1954 led, the following year, to the Labour Day parade being rebranded as the centrepiece of Moomba. An annual outdoor festival held in early March, Moomba focused on garden shows, open-air art exhibitions and, on the Yarra, various water sports.

The name 'Moomba' originated from *An Aboriginal Moomba*, a theatre production staged by the Australian Aborigines' League in 1951. At the suggestion of the league's president, Bill Onus, Melbourne City Council adopted the name for its new festival, telling Melburnians that it meant 'Let's get together and have fun'. Years later, a rumour would surface that Bill Onus had pulled a swifty, deliberately mistranslating *moomba*, which really meant 'bum', or 'up your bum'. The Onus family first confirmed then denied the story, which lives on to this day, as does Moomba. If it *was* a joke—or even if it wasn't—it's a corker. Moomba!

4:K

EMILY MCPHERSON COLLEGE
CORNER RUSSELL & VICTORIA STREETS

The stated objective of the College of Domestic Economy, which first opened in Lonsdale Street in 1907, was 'the making of good housewives'. It had grown out of an idea hatched and promoted in the women's pages of the *Herald* at a time when popular wisdom attributed a man's success in life, or otherwise, to his wife's ability to cook and keep house. The college's B-plot was to train domestic servants out of the bad and antiquated habits picked up by learning on the job. Students were 'scientifically' schooled in hygienic household management and the economical use of foodstuffs. To graduate, they had to be able to answer such posers as 'What is the difference between an aspic and a jelly?' and 'Name the parts of an ox, and how you would use them.' But so cramped were the original premises that the college could accept only thirty students at a time.

In the mid-1920s the college was granted a portion of the old Melbourne Gaol site and, thanks to a sizeable donation, built the Emily McPherson College of Domestic Economy, named in honour of the donor's wife. A caretaker's quarters left over from the gaol formed part of the new building and the bluestone wall of the exercise yard was kept intact. But with eight hundred female enrolees—and painted dazzling white—the college could not have less resembled its grim predecessor: 'Where handcuffs clanked and keys grated in locks will now be heard the pleasant clatter of china and the metallic ring of kettle, pot and pan.'

In 1927, 'Emily Mac' was officially opened by the visiting Duchess of York (later Queen Elizabeth, and eventually the Queen Mother). She wore, for the occasion, a petunia-coloured Bangkok hat and what sounds like a laundress's nightmare: a metal brocaded coat of oxidised silver with velvet lining and a collar of squirrel fur. Presented with an honorary diploma, she acknowledged it as 'a delightful memento, but one of which I am afraid I am not worthy'. Dr Ethel Osborne, chair of the college council, assured the duchess that the diploma recognised her sacrifice of 'some of the greatest moments of a mother's life'. (To accompany the duke on his tour of the Empire, she had left her infant daughter—the present Queen—at home in England, missing her first birthday.) In fact, said Dr Osborne, 'We all feel that you are particularly entitled to be regarded as an example of the best traditions in home life'—rather a ju-jitsu take on the college's usual definition of happy homemaking. Besides, you had to wonder if the duchess really could tell the difference between an aspic and a jelly.

GALLOWS

CORNER FRANKLIN & VICTORIA STREETS

Melbourne's six public executions all took place over the course of 1842. This was where the gallows stood, 'close by the walls of the new gaol…on a clear rising ground' with 'room for a concourse of ten thousand persons'—twice the population of Melbourne at the time. Tunnerminnerwait and Maulboyheenner, Aboriginal men from Van Diemen's Land convicted of murder, were the first to be hanged here.

Barred from swearing an oath on the bible,* the defendants and Aboriginal witnesses hadn't been allowed to give evidence in court. Their barrister, Redmond Barry, had called at the outset for a *jury de mediatate linguae*—literally, 'jury of the half tongue'. (The law allowed, when an 'alien' was on trial, for a jury composed of six British subjects and six of his own countrymen.) But that request was denied. And even though the all-white jury would temper its guilty verdict with a recommendation for mercy, the judge sentenced Tunnerminnerwait and Maulboyheenner to death—in order, he said, 'to deter similar transgressions'.

The Melbourne press claimed to abhor the 'disgusting' spectacle of a public execution and were 'happy to say' that the sheriff had had trouble finding someone to act as

* Indigenous people were thought to lack 'knowledge of a Supreme Being'.

hangman. Still, a hanging was as good as a fair and, by eight in the morning, thousands were crowded round the gallows, even perched in the branches of gum trees and on the unfinished walls of the gaol. By nine it was over, and by ten the bodies were taken away for burial, in unconsecrated ground outside the cemetery—now the site of Victoria Market. (See 7:B.)

Since 2016, the artwork *Standing by Tunnerminnerwait and Maulboyheenner* has marked the site of their hanging.

4:M

NED KELLY TRIAL

CORNER LA TROBE & RUSSELL STREETS

Here stood the weatherboard Supreme Court where, in 1880, bushranger Ned Kelly was tried for the murder of a policeman, one of three killed at Stringybark Creek. The accused couldn't give evidence in his own defence; only after the guilty verdict was he allowed to speak. Kelly assured the court, then, of his 'easy conscience' and said that, had he been ably defended and his evidence heard, the jury would surely have seen things his way. The judge, Sir Redmond Barry, called him blasphemous: 'You appear to revel in the idea of having put men to death.' To which Kelly replied, 'More men than I have put men to death.'

It was true: Barry was infamous as a hanging judge.

Now, he delivered the customary death sentence, ending with: 'May the Lord have mercy on your soul.' But it was Kelly who had the last word: 'I will go further than that and say *I will see you there where I go*.'

And the hex worked. Ned Kelly was hanged in the gaol alongside the courthouse on 11 November 1880. Redmond Barry died twelve days later. Where the afterlife took them and whether they met there is anyone's guess.

4:N

MELBOURNE HOSPITAL SMOKESTACK

CORNER LONSDALE & RUSSELL STREETS

At this corner, until 1948, stood the boiler house of the old Melbourne Hospital. It was seen as a landmark—literally, because of its towering chimney stack. Smokestacks had sprigged the skyline since before there were church spires, let alone skyscrapers,* but with the downturn of steam power, the city had already lost most of them. The affection Melburnians felt for the old boiler house was less about nostalgia, however, and more about the warmth from the perpetually stoked boiler, which radiated through

* The shot tower preserved under a glass cone at Melbourne Central may look like a chimney, but was actually the opposite: a vertical cooling tunnel. Blobs of molten lead dripped from the top of the tower would solidify into perfect spheres before they reached the bottom.

the red-brick walls to the footpath. The Russell Street wall, sheltered from bitter south-westerlies, was a popular spot in cold weather and bore a 'familiar smudge', decades in the making, left by the backs of all those who'd leant there.

4:O

GREEK QUARTER

LONSDALE STREET

Oyster saloons, precursors of the fish and chip shop, proliferated during the 1870s and '80s with the ready availability not just of oysters but, crucially, of ice. In 1880 not one Melbourne oyster-saloon proprietor was Greek-born; within ten years, nearly all were.

Most of those early Greek immigrants—with names like Croacos, Andrulachis, Kuvaras, Paxenos, Matoorekos, Theodossio, Mavromates and Varvarigos—came from the island of Ithaca. The first, a sailor named Andreas Lekatsas, had jumped ship in Melbourne in 1848, then knocked about on the goldfields and ended up staying away longer than Odysseus. It would be his tales of life in Victoria that sowed wanderlust in the next generation of Ithacans.

At the turn of the 1890s, Greek-run oyster saloons were plentiful in Swanston and Elizabeth streets, especially in the vicinity of Lonsdale. Only Giorgi Pappadukis had an oyster saloon here, in the part of Lonsdale Street that would eventually become the Greek quarter. By 1930 there were Greek-run clubs and cafes, fruiterers, wine shops, tailors, hairdressers and tobacconists—but not a single oyster saloon—all along this side of Lonsdale Street, from Russell to Elizabeth. And just beyond Elizabeth Street were the offices of the Ulysses Ithacan Philanthropic Society, founded by Antonios Lekatsas (Antony Lucas, see 5:G), nephew of the pioneering Andreas. The Lonsdale Street frontage of Myer's department store would displace many small shops in the 1930s, after which the Greek archipelago contracted to this stretch between Russell and Swanston streets.

Melbourne's Greek community is widely dispersed now, leaving hardly a trace here—except for each March, when Lonsdale Street hosts the Melbourne Antipodes Festival to coincide with Greek National Day.

4:P

QUEEN VICTORIA HOSPITAL

210 LONSDALE STREET

The Queen Victoria Hospital for Women took over this site when the Royal Melbourne Hospital moved out to Parkville in 1944. This entire block, from Swanston to

Russell Street, was crammed with buildings and outbuildings spanning the old hospital's hundred-year history. The main Lonsdale Street frontage was Edwardian, a uniform suite in red brick, with three towers like the one that still stands.

In the movie *On the Beach*, adapted from Nevil Shute's novel and filmed, as we've heard, in Melbourne in 1959, the city awaited the apocalypse. The Cold War had turned hot, and now lethal radiation was drifting inexorably southward, blotting out humanity degree by degree of latitude. With the end just days away, Melburnians were offered 'suicide pills'. In the movie, a medical station was set up at this gateway and hundreds of extras queued on Lonsdale Street to be issued with little white boxes labelled *Government Prescription No. 24768.*

The Queen Vic relocated to the suburbs at the end of 1980s, and all but this one tower was demolished. The rest of the block stood empty for years, and some hoped—campaigned, in fact—for it to be reserved as a public park, or even a real city square. The nearest it came to that impossible dream was the creation of a temporary skate park at the Swanston Street end for a couple of years in the '90s. Surrounded by cyclone-wire fencing, it was a joyous and virtuosic performance space, as popular with spectators as with skaters. Of course, it couldn't last.

When construction began on the site of the old Queen Vic, the project manager assured Melburnians that the new QV development would be 'a lot better than what was here before—it was just a big hole in the ground'. An inadvertent effect of the anti-big-hole ethos would be a wind-tunnel on Little Lonsdale Street that can turn any foray on foot into a mime performance. You lean into the wind, but get nowhere.

4:Q

STATE LIBRARY OF VICTORIA

SWANSTON STREET

In the absence—the perpetual absence—of a real city square, the State Library forecourt has in recent decades become Melbourne's front lawn and a rallying point for protests. It's poignant then to recall one of the final scenes in *On the Beach*, showing an empty State Library forecourt, post-apocalypse, strewn with papers under a dead grey sky.

On the lawn near La Trobe Street there's a statue of the man for whom the street was named: C. J. La Trobe, Victoria's first governor. It's a newish addition to the monumental array hereabouts and, whatever your view of public statuary, you've got to admit this one's kind of charming. For one thing, the sculptor has preserved his subject's underbite; in La Trobe's day (he came to Melbourne in 1839), an underbite was practically a sign of good breeding. What a pity he's not smiling. A contemporary wrote that La Trobe had a smile that 'might ripen a banana'. Meaning, presumably, that it was radiant like the tropical sun.

By all accounts a gentle soul, in his statue La Trobe wears a ceremonial sword. In life, his sword gave him some trouble. A town councillor tripped on it while standing on a crowded dais at one of the infant town's innumerable sod-turnings. To steady himself, he grabbed the governor's arm, then La Trobe clutched at the mayor and all three men, plus the reprehensible sword, keeled backwards off the platform, through a curtain and into the refreshment tent behind.

La Trobe's statue stands on the spot once earmarked for Captain Cook's cottage. Philanthropist Sir Russell Grimwade presented the cottage in 1934 as a gift to mark Melbourne's centenary—a well-meant gesture that provoked a fair bit of controversy. Although the cottage, transplanted from the village of Great Ayton in Yorkshire, had been home to Cook's parents in their dotage, it was doubtful that their seafaring son had ever slept a night there. He was thought to have set foot in it just once, on his return from 'discovering' Australia in 1770.

The cottage was intended to nestle 'unobtrusively' in front of the library, 'where it could be protected from souvenir hunters at night'. But mutterings about 'rubbish cluttering up the lawn' swelled to objections that 'the dreadful incongruity' of 'this squalid little building' would diminish the library's stately façade. Opposition reached such a pitch that a site in Fitzroy Gardens was settled on instead.

In pride of place on the library forecourt—right in front of the entrance steps—stands a statue of Sir Redmond Barry, erected after his death. Though Barry had played a founding role in several of Melbourne's civic institutions, the Public Library (now State Library Victoria) was his spiritual home. If Barry was...morally complex, then the library reflected his finer inclinations.

When it opened, in 1856, Melbourne's public library was recognised as 'the *only* public library in the world, in the true sense'. Unlike those in Britain on which it was modelled, this one was open to all, male or female, aged fourteen or older—provided their hands were clean (a handbasin and soap were provided). Elsewhere, admission to libraries was limited to men over twenty-one who held a reader's ticket, which required references from respectable property-owners. In the Melbourne Public Library, the shelves were open, allowing readers to choose books for themselves, unlike other libraries where only staff could access the shelves and books were issued on request (which would have been tricky since, to begin with, there was no catalogue). Hermann Beckler arrived in Melbourne in 1859 and wrote home to his brother in Bavaria:

> *Dear Karl, this is a wonderful, free, civilised land. There is no-one checking to see whether anyone is stealing a book. The best book in the library is too good for nobody.*

Even so, in the library's early decades, there were repeated calls for a ticket system to be introduced and complaints about rough handling or theft of books by readers 'unfit' for admittance. But the great and immovable obstacle to any stiffening of the library rules was none other than Redmond Barry, head of the trustees.* He liked to boast that 'Our Library is free in every sense.' It was Barry who, in 1856, proposed the rule admitting readers as young as fourteen, a rule he later defended thus: 'If it were necessary to deprive people of seven years' reading, it would be better to strike off the seven years at the *other* end, and disqualify people at sixty-three.' Barry himself, at that point, had just turned sixty-four.

For more than century, Redmond Barry's portly likeness in front of the State Library was perpetually crowned with a crust of guano that appeared as a ghostly approximation of the cap worn by a judge issuing a death sentence. Now, though, a pair of antenna-like prongs deters pigeons from settling, and crapping, on Sir Redmond's morally complex barnet.

---

* Before Melbourne had a public library, Barry ran one in his own home (see 6:D).

WALK 5

PANTALOONED FOR ETERNITY

In which we trace Burke and Wills' posthumous peregrinations and the evolution of the arcade

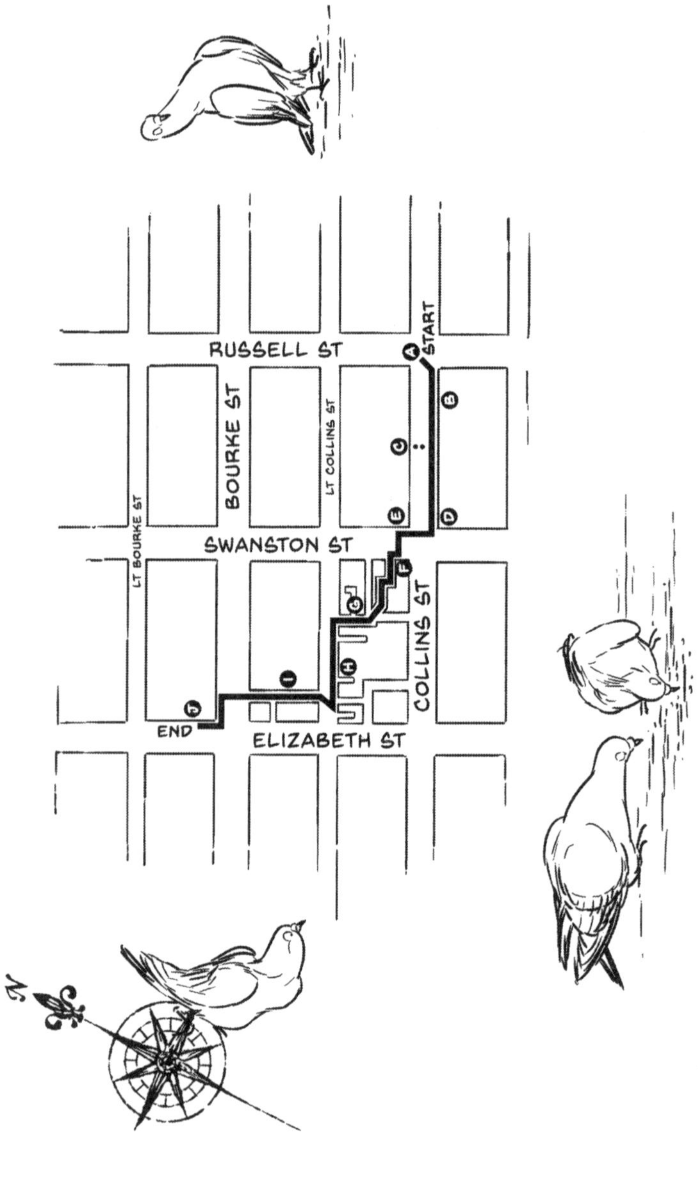
RUSSELL ST
START
A
B
C
D
E
F
G
H
I
J
END
BOURKE ST
LT COLLINS ST
LT BOURKE ST
SWANSTON ST
COLLINS ST
ELIZABETH ST
N

BURKE & WILLS MONUMENT

CORNER COLLINS & RUSSELL STREETS

For twenty-one years two dead men haunted the middle of this intersection, impeding the free flow of traffic. From this elevated spot the memorial statue of Burke and Wills (see 4:E) enjoyed the kind of vantage point the two men had sorely lacked on their ill-fated expedition. This wasn't the preferred site for the monument to begin with—a plaster prototype was trialled in other locations around the city, but they lacked the visual punch of this one. With 'the slope of the street rising sharply from the intersection of Swanston Street [said the *Argus*], the effect is very fine'.

Sculptor Charles Summers cast the figures in bronze—Wills seated, Burke standing—in his Collins Street studio, close by. Twice as large as life and pantalooned for eternity, they were unveiled in 1865. On the granite pedestal, bronze panels depicted scenes from the expedition, with a decorative trim of nardoo, an aquatic fern that likely contributed to the explorers' deaths. Marooned at Cooper Creek, they'd observed that nardoo was an Indigenous staple: the spores were ground and made into bread or gruel. But eating nothing *but* nardoo, it turns out, causes beriberi. Why then would the sculptor taunt the bronze Burke and Wills with a frieze of nardoo? Because the plant was thought, at the time, to have prolonged the lives of the

starving pair—their nearest thing to a saviour.

Whether in spite or because of its prominence, the monument got a reputation as 'the only place' in the city for assignations. Marcus Clarke, a wry observer of the city's social currents (it was he who popularised the expression 'doing the Block'), wrote of the scene at the monument:

> *Often has my tender heart been bruised at the sight of half-a-dozen young persons of either sex shivering round its plinth on a cool autumn evening, all pretending to be rapturously occupied in gazing at the bas-relief.*

Fergus Hume, on the opening page of his bestselling *The Mystery of a Hansom Cab* (1886), recounts a cab driver's statement to the police, beginning: 'At the hour of one o'clock in the morning, he was driving down Collins Street East, when, as he was passing the Burke and Wills monument, he was hailed by a gentleman standing at the corner…' By the time the cab reached St Kilda, its passenger was dead. That same year, the advent of cable trams in Collins Street meant the displacement of Burke and Wills (and the beginning of the end for hansom cabs). The monument's new home in Spring Street would be likewise uprooted eighty-seven years later for the construction of Parliament station. Burke and Wills bivouac'd in Carlton Gardens before putting down roots in the (then) new city square, where chlorinated spray from a fountain would damage their bronze patina. After a cut-and-polish, they were re-sited, high and dry, at the city square's Collins Street corner.

When work began on the Metro tunnel project, the monument went into storage, for a planned return to the same corner once the new Town Hall station is complete. But there's a push to see Burke and Wills restored instead to a more elevated spot—ideally, on the grounds of the Royal Society of Victoria, the august body that sent the pair north in the first place. Given the backlash against colonialist monuments, the city council may well be glad to unload Burke and Wills. One thing's for sure: their journey isn't over yet.

5:B

T&G BUILDING

147 COLLINS STREET

Madame Carole, clairvoyant physician and medical mesmerist, practised her healing arts on this spot for a few years around 1860. Under her real name, Caroline Harper Dexter, she'd claimed to be the first woman in Britain to adopt bloomers: voluminous harem-style pants worn under a short (calf-length) skirt. Before coming to Australia in 1855, she'd toured England and Scotland, lecturing on 'rational dress' and corset reform—and modelling the scandalous bloomer outfit. In Melbourne she apprenticed herself to a homeopathic doctor (of whom there were as many practising in Collins Street as there were mainstream medicos), then started her own practice, ministering mainly to women and children.

Madame Carole's methods incorporated herbal medicine and mesmerism, or 'magnetic sleep'. As a side-hustle, at the same address, she ran the Hygiene Institute, dispensing (mainly) commonsense instruction on topics such as dressing appropriately for hot weather and how to avoid 'impure air'.

Caroline Dexter was a writer as well as a healer. In 1861, with her friend Harriet Clisby, she issued *The Interpreter*, the first Australian magazine published by women. What it aimed to interpret were 'the thoughts, feelings and sentiments of all those whose interest is the advancement of humanity', via poetry and serial fiction, essays on 'Beauty' and 'A Phrenology of Dreams', profiles of women from history and 'Our Medical Page'. The first issue (there would be only two) carried a full page of testimonials for Madame Carole's efficacy 'as a curative operator in many of those dangerous and debilitating diseases which are peculiarly incident to females'.

Harriet Clisby left soon after to study medicine in New York, graduating among the first batch of female doctors anywhere. Madame Carole, meanwhile, married an adoring younger man with a big house at Brighton, where she reinvented herself as Carrie Lynch, patron of the arts.

Fifty years later on this spot stood Burke and Wills Chambers, its three floors tenanted chiefly by music teachers and elocutionists, along with a wigmaker, a stamp vendor, an electro-masseuse and just enough dentists to remind you this was Collins Street. But, after the site was swallowed in 1927 by the T&G building, dentists would so rule the roost that it was dubbed the Tooth and Gum building. During construction, though, the ten-storey T&G (headquarters of Temperance and General, an insurance firm) was known as the Touch and Go—a comment on the reckless speed with which it went up.

In theory, there was still a strict limit on the height of city buildings. (See 2:E.) But since the early 1920s, ornamental towers had been permitted, to unlimited height, on top of the forty-metre maximum. The result was predictable: a craze for towers—the taller the better. The T&G's towers (it had two)* added seven metres to its height and, with its elevated position and dazzling white façade, made it easily the most prominent feature on the city skyline.

* When the T&G building was extended in 1939, one tower was pulled down and the remaining one made taller.

BAPTIST CHURCH / ATHENAEUM / MECHANICS' INSTITUTE

COLLINS STREET

On this stretch of Collins Street, between Swanston and Russell, the slope of the Eastern Hill was originally even steeper than it is today. Major earthworks reduced the gradient in 1849. But the Baptist Church, with steps leading to an entrance high above the street, preserves a relic of the hill-slope before it was 'cut down'. The church was built in 1861, but on the same site—and at the same height—as its 1845 predecessor.

Where the Athenaeum Theatre stands was once the Melbourne Mechanics' Institute. Primarily a lecture hall and lending library for tradespeople and workers, it was part of an international movement of self-improvement that helped create an educated middle class. As an instructional venue with no ties to traditional seats of knowledge and learning—the university, the Royal Society—the Mechanics' Institute could act as a sounding house for new ideas, including those on the metaphysical spectrum that didn't qualify as mainstream science or philosophy or religion, but one day just might.

Harriet Clisby, to raise money for her passage to New

York, gave a lecture at the Mechanics' titled: 'A Night with Spirits'. In it, she presented compelling accounts of table-turning, spirit-rapping and other manifestations, and defended a belief in spiritualism on moral and spiritual grounds—all 'with a propriety of language which could have offended very few of her audience'. Lecturing here on von Reichenbach's theory of animal magnetism, Madame Carole reminded *her* audience of 'the ridicule originally heaped upon the idea of propelling vessels by steam'. 'It is no easy task,' she said, 'to become the pioneer of a doctrine so startling and yet so scantily investigated as to be still in the dark stream of scepticism.'

5:D

CITY SQUARE

CORNER COLLINS & SWANSTON STREETS

When Melbourne's street grid was drawn up, ahead of the first land sale in 1837, no space was allocated for a public square. Surveyor Hoddle wasn't to blame: his proposal for 'a very handsome square' was overruled. British cities just then were seeing mass demonstrations by Chartists calling for political and social reforms. A public square, the thinking went, wouldn't just give the mob a place to gather but would 'encourage democracy'—not a good thing in a far-flung finger of the Empire.

Melbourne wouldn't have a designated city square until 1980. To make space, all the buildings, laneways and arcades between here and Flinders Lane were rubbed out over the course of the '70s. A swathe of the city—Queen's Walk, Regent Place, the Cathedral Hotel where the murderer Deeming shed his skin—was laid to waste. And was it worth it? When finally done, the city square felt like the over-determined afterthought it was. In the decades since, it's been repeatedly tinkered with and encroached upon, never given a chance to grow an identity of its own. Let's hope the new Town Hall station will make it…if not exactly a city square, at least something other than a void.

Among the justifications for the naming of AC/DC Lane was that it runs parallel to the route followed by the band's 1976 music video for 'It's a Long Way to the Top (If You Wanna Rock 'n' Roll)'. Well, this was the route: Swanston Street. Separated by a couple of city blocks, the parallelism seems pretty spurious.

The boys (and they *were* boys then, not golfing geezers) performed the song on a flatbed truck travelling south on Swanston Street, like a feral Moomba float. Swanston Street, back then, was one of the city's main traffic arteries and, starting from Bourke Street in morning peak hour, the truck made slow headway: by the time it reached this point, Bon Scott was squawking the last chorus. After the bagpipe fade-out (by members of the Rats of Tobruk pipe band—plus Bon, faking it) the lads dismounted for an encore at the makeshift city square, with the Regent Theatre's side wall as a backdrop.

The video, filmed for *Countdown*, ABC-TV's legendary pop music showcase, took its cue from the song's opening lyric: *Ridin' down the highway*...But why choose Swanston Street? After all, the title suggests an uphill climb. Why not the Collins Street hill instead? Sure, they might have lost the drum kit off the back. But hey, it's a long way to the top...

There used to be a fountain here, right in the middle of the Collins and Swanston streets intersection. Installed to celebrate the Yan Yean water supply in 1859, the Victoria fountain was a beacon to street urchins, stray dogs and thirsty beasts of burden, and presented such an obstacle to traffic that it lasted just five years.

TOWN HALL

N-E CORNER COLLINS & SWANSTON STREETS

One of my favourite images of nineteenth-century Melbourne shows a portion of the thousands-strong crowd that assembled round this spot in 1867 to witness the laying of the foundation stone for the town hall. (A foundation-stone ceremony was the next best thing to a hanging.) Performing the honours was Prince Alfred, Queen Victoria's second son and this city's first royal visitor, and Melburnians were climbing over each other to get a glimpse of him. For dignitaries, there were temporary grandstands in Collins and Swanston streets, but the common ruck filled the roadway and hung off every verandah and rooftop.

Melburnians took to Prince Alfred, a Royal Navy man who spurned glove-wearing. And the prince liked Melbourne—better than Sydney, anyway, where he was shot by a would-be assassin. He had a favourite bordello in Stephen (Exhibition) Street and made himself at home at the exclusive Melbourne Club. He paid the city an unofficial return visit in 1869 and, one lunchtime, the 'now-familiar figure of His Royal Highness' sauntered down from the Melbourne Club to ceremonially set in place—with his 'honest, bare, brown, working-looking hand'—a carved stone capping the town hall clock-tower.

This time there was no crowd, no grandstand; HRH was just another figure in the scaffolding.

5:F

MANCHESTER UNITY BUILDING & ARCADE

CORNER COLLINS & SWANSTON STREETS

This corner first became a household name to Melburnians as Germain Nicholson's. One of the things the pioneer grocer sold was coffee, and in 1845 he installed a machine to roast and grind the beans by steam power. People would gather at the store's Swanston Street window to see and smell the machine in action, and demand for coffee soared. Plus, the shop stayed toasty warm in winter. Come summer, the heat from the steam engine would have sent Nicholson's stock rancid so the roaster-grinder sat idle and coffee fiends had to make do with tea.

As gateway to The Block—that byword of Melbourne boom-time swank—Germain Nicholson's corner was a shabby embarrassment by the time the old building was pulled down in 1884. 'Few will regret to learn that it is at last to disappear, to make room for a block in unison with the noble site—probably superior for business purposes to any in the colonies.'

When the four-storey Nicholson's Chambers went up,

the flagship corner shop was occupied by jeweller Stewart Dawson. Stewart Dawson's would come to rival 'under the clocks' at Flinders Street station, its wide verandah opposite the town hall clock making it the ideal rendezvous. When its turn for demolition came, the *Herald* weighed 'the disappearance of a Melbourne landmark' against the promise of 'something bigger and more magnificent' and concluded: 'Sentiment is rarely in step with the march of progress.'

The wrecking of Stewart Dawson's verandah began, with a fanfare, at midnight on New Year's Day, 1932. The construction of a twelve-storey (plus tower) Art Deco show stopper in its place was meant to signal the beginning of the end of the Depression in Melbourne. To construct a building of that magnitude would normally have taken around two years, but such was 'the willing spirit of the workmen' that the Manchester Unity went up at the unheard-of rate of one floor per week. It sure didn't look like a rush job when it was finished, though. Heralded as 'The Wonder Building', it was finished with intricate detailing—including an ornamental tower half as high as the building itself—and fitted with every mod con. The claim that 'This ever-famous corner has become still more famous' was no mere swagger.

If the pages of the Arabian Nights opened and the magic carpet floated into Collins Street, Melbourne could not watch with greater awe.

The main attraction of the Manchester Unity building on the day it opened in September 1932 was its escalator, the city's first. It took about half a minute to convey passengers from arcade level to the mezzanine, not quite 14 metres. But Melburnians were entranced. On that first day, more than sixty thousand 'escalatees' took the ride. The *Herald*'s reporter on the spot identified four stages in 'the Democratic and Modern Game of Escalating', the last being 'The Seasoned Stage', when the escalatee 'steps off at the top and hurries down the stationary stairway to take another ride'. That's right: there was (and is) no 'down' escalator. Melbourne wasn't ready for it.

And speaking of going up...When stockings were in short supply after the Second World War (the Yanks having all gone home), you could leave your precious nylons for invisible mending, here in the arcade, at the Ladderless Hosiery depot.

5:G

HOWEY PLACE

THROUGH TO LITTLE COLLINS STREET

Howey Place has always felt to me like the heart of the city. Out of the way but close to everything, with multiple points of entry and divergence. It's outdoors yet sheltered from the weather and is wide enough that you can dawdle without blocking traffic. And a million things have happened here.

For instance, fires. Howey Place and its offshoots had their share. In fact, to firefighters, this was 'one of the danger spots of the city'. There were workshops and factories tucked away, kitchens at the rear of Swanston Street restaurants and hotels and, facing Howey Place, a printing works with paper to burn. And the difficulty in fighting fires in this quarter was partly due to the glass roof overhead, which created a flue, hindered ladders and hoses, and was liable to shatter in extreme heat.

Originally an ordinary right-of-way, Howey Place was arcade-ified with that roof around 1908. Nearly directly opposite Howey Place on Little Collins Street was the rear entrance of Cole's Book Arcade. (The main entrance, with its trademark rainbow, faced Bourke Street.)

When the enterprising E. W. Cole acquired a second shop in Collins Street and the Howey Place printworks, he came up with the idea of roofing over the right-of-way, renaming it Cole's Walk and claiming it as a continuation of his Book Arcade, linking the Bourke and Collins Street branches. To encourage people to linger (and also to read more) he had 'Instructive Pictures'—pages from the illustrated newspapers—pasted up on the walls of Cole's Walk, 'fresh and free every week'.

Cole had started in bookselling with a barrow at the Eastern Market; now he boasted that his Book Arcade stocked a million books. Passionate about many things—racial equality, the power of humour, mechanised flight, communicating with monkeys—he had his most enduring credo posted on placards all through the Book Arcade: 'Read the books. No one asked to buy.'

In 1909, women with money to burn made a beeline to Howey Place, where La Chevonde hair salon had the exclusive Australian licence to Nestlé's permanent wave process. 'The talk of feminine Europe,' said the adverts; 'Over 1500 heads already waved'—*in the world*, that was. By the end of the year that number had doubled, after which they stopped counting.

Charles Nessler had perfected the perming process in 1906, but not before his wife Katharina had her scalp scorched and all her hair frizzled off. This was at least ten years before bobbed hair became a thing, and most women still had waist-length hair. The look they were after wasn't curly, but merely crimped. How enticing La Chevonde's adverts must have sounded:

> *Just think of having your hair wavy for a whole year—no curling pins, no fierce plaits, no horrible tongs. Impervious to all such exigencies as hot weather, windy days, damp atmosphere, or salt water.*

And they emphasised—always in capitals—that Nestlé's process was ABSOLUTELY HARMLESS. What did it entail? First, the hair was wound onto sixteen brass rollers, around which were wrapped flannel bandages soaked in a secret solution. Over the curlers went asbestos cones, which were poked into an array of heated metal tubes suspended, chandelier-style, overhead. (Nessler's experiments on Katharina had shown that twenty kilograms of hardware could not be borne by follicles alone.) The process took several hours and cost five guineas—a fortune! A home-perm kit could be had for two guineas, and pretty soon a kitchen-science version did the rounds, calling for borax, gum arabic and spirits of camphor and adventure.

La Chevonde's exclusive right to the Nestlé perm lasted just a couple of years. But, together with E. W. Cole's glass roof and tarmacking of the cobblestones, it seems to have raised the tone and profile of Howey Place. A few years on, a visitor from Adelaide would single it out as 'a revelation, honeycombed with tiny shops selling frocks, hats, home-made cakes, or imitation jewellery'. ('Imitation jewellery' might sound like a take-down, but it signalled 'not-your-mother's jewellery'.) Why, in the 1920s, Le Louvre (see 1:A) would make its start here.

Over the course of the 1920s and '30s, one side of Howey Place was completely remade. It was hollowed out all the way back to Swanston Street in preparation first, for the Capitol Theatre (with Capitol House above), then for a string of other fine new buildings facing the town hall. Workers levelling the site for the Capitol were astounded to find a wooden picket fence standing upright more than a metre below the surface. One of Melbourne's earliest dwellings must have stood here: removed, and its fence buried, when the ground was raised to the level of Swanston Street. Here too, in 1921, the famed sign of Whelan the Wrecker was born. In one of the buildings under demolition, Jim Whelan's wrecking crew scratched the words WHELAN THE WRECKER IS HERE on the exposed black-painted wall of a photographer's darkroom. A day or two later the wall was gone, but the words and the sign they inspired would become as ubiquitously Melbourne as Four 'n' Twenty pies.

Among the Swanston Street buildings pulled down to make way for the Capitol was the three-storey Town Hall Café, belonging to Antony Lucas (Antonios Lekatsas, from Ithaca—see 4:O). Lucas retained an interest in the Capitol in the shape of the Ambassadors Café in the building's basement. The Ambassadors could be entered from Swanston Street or Howey Place; an after-hours nightclub, the Corona, situated at the rear of the café used only the latter entrance. The Corona was fitted out on the lines of a Continental cabaret, with 'roseate' walls and plush maroon upholstery. Under the sign of a huge cigar, the club fostered an exclusive clientele of theatrical types and 'social lights'. Dame Nellie Melba was among the in-crowd at the club's 'opening jazz'; billiard champion Walter Lindrum's idea of winding down was a foxtrot at the Corona. Harry Bennett's Diamonds were the Corona's house-band, and most nights' entertainment would include an exhibition of dances like the Black Bottom and Lindy Hop. At midnight, revellers would fly coloured balloons from their wrists, then 'beguile' the hours till closing, some time before dawn. The off-street entrance doubtless added to the club's allure.

To at least one snooty social scenester, though, the Corona Club ranked as no better than provincial:

> *One would hardly have thought that Melbourne society people were so pleasure starved as to hail with joy a quasi public hall and dancing on Sunday morning. But one can never tell.*

That was in 1928. A year later the economy crashed, and with it the Corona Club.

So rowdy was the 1948 annual conference of the Housewives' Association, held in Halladale House on Howey Place, that attendees had to be reminded to behave 'like decent women'. (Press coverage hinted at infiltration by socialist agitators.) The three-day conference was marked by calls for action on such issues as rent control, child care, a national campaign for peace, and home delivery of bread.

When a Mr Evans, manager of the Metropolitan Gas Co., came to address the assembled housewives about the high cost of gas, a policeman was posted in Howey Place. No riot eventuated, though the women did hold the gas man's feet to the flames, accusing him of 'skirting around' the issue and of being 'out to make profits'. 'Isn't it time the industry was nationalised?' demanded a Mrs Bell of Camberwell (not a suburb usually synonymous with leftism). That afternoon's *Herald* reported Mr Evans' ordeal under the headline 'Women Heckle on Gas'.

My fondest Howey Place memory is of Julius Geiger Shoes, a chaotic, pocket-sized shop so *packed* with shoes that there was barely room to sit and try a pair on. The window display set the vibe: not a millimetre of space went to waste. Accompanying each sample shoe—women's only, but in endless variety—was a hand-lettered price card. And the prices were much lower than other shoe shops' in that era before cheap Chinese imports. Most of Julius Geiger's stock came from Europe. I remember a pair of two-tone knee-length boots, made in Poland from the softest leather and bought at Geiger's for a song. (The stacked heels had a tendency to snap off but, hey, were women's shoes ever made for walking?)

I'd have had a soft spot for Julius Geiger's, I think, even if I'd never stepped inside. Often when I'd pass this way the shop would be closed—as shops more often were then, with trading hours tightly regulated—but I'd linger for what seemed like hours, scanning the window display like it was one of E. W. Cole's Instructive Pictures.

5:H

LITTLE COLLINS STREET → ELIZABETH STREET

This stretch of Little Collins hasn't always been a shopping street. For a long time it was dedicated mainly to the metal trades, hazy with weird-smelling smoke and clangorous with sounds of metal on metal. The iron framework and lacework of Cole's Howey Place roof would, very likely, have been fashioned right here in the neighbourhood. Along the street and its offshooting alleys* were (let me list

* Take a look at a detailed map of the CBD and you'll see that the block bounded by Elizabeth, Collins, Swanston and Little Collins is threaded through with more laneways than any other in the city.

them): tinsmiths, ironmongers and founders, safe makers, wire workers, locksmiths, bell hangers, scale makers and brassfitters, together with, oddly, Melbourne's only two importers of corks.*

There were also a couple of assay works, where ore was chemically tested to determine how much pure metal it contained. One was in Bull Alley (now Balcombe Place), at the rear of Clarke & Sons, from the 1850s one of the city's leading gold brokers.† In the decades before Melbourne got its own branch of the Royal Mint (see 6:I), gold was assayed and smelted into ingots at the Bull Alley works. So much Victorian gold passed through Clarke & Sons' premises that old Mr Clarke, speaking when the building came to be demolished in 1888, put the aggregate value at £100 million. You can bet that when the floors were pulled up, the dirt underneath was sifted and scoured for fugitive gold dust.

Replacing Clarke & Sons was the (now) endearingly grimy City of Melbourne building, named not for the city council but for the short-lived City of Melbourne Building Society, one of the many land-boom outfits undone by the 1890s depression.

Hairdresser Frederick Radford, in 1903, had a saloon

---

* Of no small interest to a one-time cork expert like me (see 4:C).

† Another assay works had its entrance in Brown Alley. One of two laneways by that name in the CBD, in 2007 it was redesignated Dame Edna Place, in honour of that cringeworthy Melburnian, Dame Edna Everage.

(sic) in one of the City of Melbourne building's Elizabeth Street shopfronts and another in Bull Alley, which he ran as a school for barbers. In fact, it was a racket. Radford—who sometimes went by 'Professor' Radford, the sure sign of a conman—took half a dozen 'scholars' at a time, charging them as much as £40 for their training. He promised they'd have 'real live individuals from the highways and the byways' to practise on, but mainly they clipped and shaved one another. After a few weeks, Radford would claim there was too little business to support them, and they'd be dismissed—even as he was advertising for fresh trainees.

For a while, his wife kept four female scholars at her 'pretty little saloon' up near Howey Place. An advert in one of the society papers stated, by way of credentials: 'Mrs Radford is the wife of Professor Radford, who introduced lady barbers into Melbourne.' Perhaps he had. Between bouts of barbering and insolvency, the Professor had also practised as a medical herbalist, or eclectic botanist, offering women 'relief from all complaints incidental to the sex' which, like 'restoring regularity', was universally recognised as code for abortion.

By the twentieth century, the metal trades on Little Collins Street would refine towards watch- and jewellery-making, befitting proximity to The Block and the arcadian cross-currents of fashionable Melbourne. But in 1870, when the Royal Arcade opened, patrons of its bijou shops and fallalery must have found it disconcerting to step out into not a retail street but an industrial quarter.

5:1

THE BEADLE

ROYAL ARCADE → BOURKE STREET

Grouped at the Little Collins Street end of the Royal Arcade were originally a fountain, aquarium and fernery, concealing the entrance to a yard where the 'offices' (i.e. toilets) were situated. And opposite the yard, just past the fernery, were the quarters of the Arcade beadle.

A beadle was an old-style civic functionary responsible for keeping order. The archetypal beadle was the cruel and puffed-up Mr Bumble, who oversaw the parish workhouse-cum-orphanage in *Oliver Twist*. Melbourne's earlier arcade, the Queen's, which opened in 1853, had a beadle, 'constantly promenading the Arcade to keep out all improper characters, thus enabling ladies to make their purchases without fear of molestation'. But by 1870, a beadle in Melbourne was seen as an anachronism.

The *Age* condemned 'this piece of flunkery' as 'offensive' and 'not likely to last'. And, 'It speaks little for colonial advancement,' said one young fellow who'd been told by the beadle to 'move on'. The beadle himself, Frederick Batchelder, was tall and portly and, by all accounts, suffused with self-importance. He was an object of derision from the start:

> *This great civic dignitary has been appointed, invested with an awe-inspiring and gorgeous livery...Let naughty little boys beware.*

Batchelder was decked out, Regency-style, in gold-trimmed blue and red livery, with a glossy black top hat and 'formidable' cane. *Melbourne Punch* lampooned him in a series of cartoons: 'The Beadle quelling a rebellion' (he canes a small boy); 'The Beadle after dinner. A child might play with him now' (he snoozes at his post).

The beadle and his brass-tipped cane failed to keep pickpockets at bay, however. Within days of the opening, a policeman was assigned to patrol the arcade daily, and two on Saturday nights. But Batchelder's duties weren't confined to crowd control. It was his job to spray the glass roof with water on hot days and to keep the arcade's aquarium well-stocked. (In pursuance of which duty he inadvertently bought goldfish stolen from the Treasury Gardens.) And once, defending his employer's interests in a dispute over some cut flowers, he almost destroyed one of the arcade's shops:

> *The beadle is big, and the shop is small, and, in the course of the evolutions incidental to such a conflict*

> *as that in which he was engaged, he knocked down and killed a bullfinch, smashed an aquarium, and injured other property.*

As well as a florist's, the Royal Arcade's twenty-two shops included a music seller's, a toy shop, a bird shop, a picture seller's, several fancy-goods shops and two photographers. Or, as Marcus Clarke put it, 'It abounds with shops where one can purchase things one doesn't want.' Clarke praised the arcade as 'an admirable spot for assignations'—more sheltered than the Burke and Wills monument, and less conspicuous. In fact, 'It has everything that can be desired, even a beadle.'

Batchelder, in his finery, remained a fixture of the Royal Arcade for sixteen years. And long after that, small boys grown old would fondly remember their one-time foe, the man they'd called 'the Beetle'.

GPO STEPS
ELIZABETH STREET

This was one of the spots on flood-prone Elizabeth Street where water was most inclined to pool during Melbourne's early decades. The suggestion of a ferry service was only half-meant as a joke and, after a man *and his horse* were drowned here one night, there were calls to install life-buoys 'the whole length of the post office coast'.

Elizabeth Street being the city's low-point, topographically speaking, it wasn't just rainwater that flowed down to gather here. Industrial sludge and overflow from privies also seeped downhill to muddy the roadway and settle in pools under buildings. When a row of old shops was demolished to make way for the Royal Arcade—almost level with Elizabeth Street—'a horrid deposit of stinking mud' was exposed, 'which accounts for the musty kind of odour always pervading so many of the places of business'. At the post office, seepage from privies in a neighbouring laneway festered under the floor. Postal clerks fainted from the stench and customers habitually held handkerchiefs to their faces.

The old post office had been built in 1841 to cater to a growing population, but was in no way equipped to handle the volume of mail and patrons that the gold rush brought to Melbourne. In 1850, the year before the Victorian gold discoveries, something like two hundred thousand letters and three hundred thousand newspapers passed through the Melbourne post office. Within three years, those numbers would increase ten-fold. There were no postmen or pillar boxes, so that anyone sending or receiving mail had to queue—for hours—at the post office. Many of them, passing through Melbourne on their way to or from the goldfields, would have been queuing in the hope of collecting mail addressed simply to *J. Blow, Melbourne.*

In the lottery-like atmosphere of the gold rush, the post office struggled to keep hold of its staff. Those who stayed had to work twelve-hour days six days a week, in what must have been a postal clerk's nightmare. After witnessing the sight of clerks knee-deep in mail, one customer damned Melbourne's post office as 'a disgrace to the British character'.

A flag raised over the clock tower signalled the arrival of a mail ship from England. Inside the post office it meant chaos, but outside there'd be a fairground atmosphere. Thousands would be milling around, abuzz with anticipation or flush with news from home. Relatives and neighbours last seen ten thousand miles away would meet by accident in the crowds spilling onto the roadways. There'd be pie-carts, lemonade sellers, a brass band—and pickpockets aplenty.

For the filming of *On the Beach,* the GPO was cast as the Department of Navy. Anthony Perkins, playing a young naval officer, displayed recklessness in the face of that radioactive cloud by dismounting from a north-bound tram *between stops* and dodging traffic before bounding up these steps to receive his orders. Luckily, he was in the Free Tram Zone (and it was 1959), or he'd have been collared by that latter-day beadle, the Myki enforcement officer.

In the *Encyclopedia of Melbourne* (page 293), I read that 'Sixteen species of frog...can be found within 50 metres of the Melbourne General Post Office.' Astounded, I looked again—it said *50 kilometres*. It's not such a stretch of the imagination, though: the damp locale would surely suit them to a tee.

WALK 6

DR LOVE

In which we see where hot passions can lead and discover what Melbourne's made of

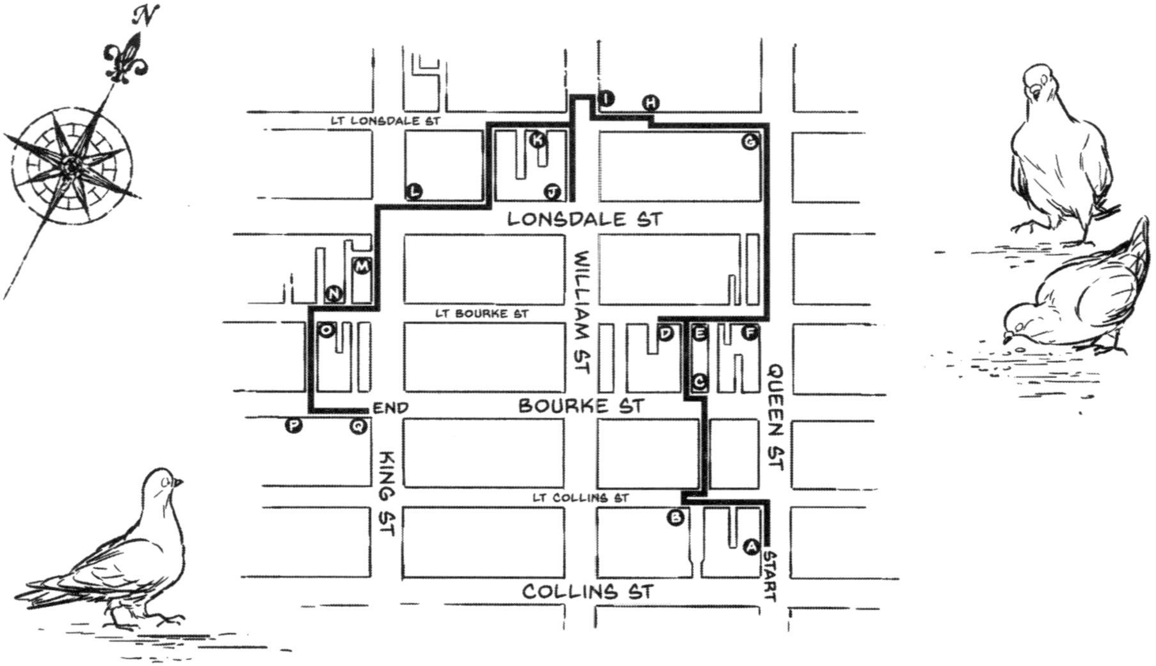
N
LT LONSDALE ST
LONSDALE ST
LT BOURKE ST
WILLIAM ST
BOURKE ST
LT COLLINS ST
COLLINS ST
KING ST
QUEEN ST
START
END
A
B
C
D
E
F
G
H
I
J
K
L
M
N
O
P
Q

6:A

HOTEL DE FRANCE

101 QUEEN STREET

Auguste Debeaux, in 1860, opened the Hotel de France in a double-fronted brick building on this spot. On one side of the central hallway was the bar; across the hall was a restaurant serving French and English meals. The French consul was a patron, and it was said to be the only place of its kind in Melbourne that 'a respectable female could go into and be treated with politeness and civility'.

Debeaux opened a second Hotel de France on the riverside at South Yarra, surrounded by orchards and a vineyard, which floods swept through late in 1863. Just weeks later, his Queen Street hotel collapsed.

The building, two storeys high with attic rooms above, had been put up in a hurry in 1852, when the inrush of gold-seekers put the squeeze on Melbourne lodgings. Skilled tradesmen were in short supply just then (most had gone off to the diggings) and the building was shaky from the start. Several times over the years its foundations had been shored up but, even so, its front wall slumped noticeably in the middle. The hope was that the buildings on either side would hold it up. And they did—until twenty past two on a Sunday morning in January 1864.

The Hotel de France was full for the New Year weekend,

with the front bedroom upstairs occupied by a honeymoon couple. With a loud warning crack, the whole front of the hotel—two rooms deep—peeled off. One report had the newlyweds and their bed thrown into the middle of the street; another had them escape by the stairs. Either way, they found themselves in Queen Street, showered by bricks, half-blinded by dust and 'almost in a state of nudity' (it was a stifling hot night). The Hotel de France was a write-off and Monsieur Debeaux 'a heavy loser by the occurrence'. For him, insolvency followed and, not long after, death at the age of forty-two. As for the newlyweds...after a start like that, married life must have seemed pretty humdrum.

6:B

STALBRIDGE CHAMBERS

443 LITTLE COLLINS STREET

This section of Little Collins Street was early on designated Chancery Lane. As in the London street of that name, barristers and solicitors congregated there, even though it wasn't situated particularly close to any court of law. Many of the offices that swarmed with wig-wearers and scriveners had been built as houses in Melbourne's early years, when this was the big end of town. Their dingy unpretentiousness, forty years on, was said to reflect 'the conservatism peculiar to the legal profession'.

Traditionally, 'chambers' were rooms occupied by barristers. Over the course of the nineteenth century, though, the term busted out to lend class to any office building. Chambers proliferated in the Melbourne CBD during the booming 1880s, increasing in number from sixteen to seventy. Stalbridge Chambers, built in 1890, was among the grandest, and put to shame the old, low-slung buildings that still characterised Chancery Lane. Seven storeys high and close to the summit of the city's western hill, it stood out, midway between the law courts on William Street and the financial district of Collins and Queen.

Nearly all Melbourne's chambers seem to have been named with the mother country in mind. Stalbridge Chambers was typical, honouring British government minister and peer Baron Stalbridge (né Grosvenor, also a chambers' name). Sturdy-sounding 'lounge-suite' names were preferable to distinctive ones—let alone any hint of local colour. What a contrast to the goldfields, where gullies and reefs were readily dubbed Eureka, Moonlight, Kangaroo and Perseverance (and Dead Horse and Humbug). Maybe names like those translated better to hotels than to professional chambers; still, it seems a pity that the same nomenclative spirit didn't extend to the metropolis. Odd names out among Melbourne chambers were Burke and Wills, Batman and Apollo—and Planet Chambers, named for the Planet Permanent Building Society (not so permanent, as it turned out).

Occupying offices in chambers along Chancery Lane in the 1890s were Misses Mott, French, Harriott, Crisp and Nankivell, all of them typewriters. (That's right: the operator shared a name with her machine.) Some of them also wrote shorthand, which had only recently been relegated to a female profession. Until the 1880s shorthand had been the domain, mainly, of reporters—in parliament, the courts and for newspapers—and nearly all of them were men. For a brief time thirty years earlier, though, shorthand had also been an idealistic medium, allied with the movement for educational and language reform, even—as a form of phonetics—a step towards a universal language.

Harriet Clisby (see 5:B), before she was a doctor or friend to Madame Carole, had practised and taught phonography, as shorthand was then known. She even edited a magazine, the *Southern Phonographic Harmonia*, published in Melbourne and printed entirely in shorthand. In the 'new era' that followed the initial chaos of the gold rush, predicted Clisby, 'truth and goodness will be in the ascendant and the phonetic cause will flourish'. Her idealism reflected that of Isaac Pitman, the inventor of shorthand, who believed that the time it saved might, in effect, add ten or fifteen years to a lifespan. In the 1850s, Clisby chafed at the limited vocations open to women, so would surely have been glad to see so many employed, by the end of the century, on the fringes of commerce and the law—albeit still in a handmaiden capacity. In fact, she *did* see it. Shorthand had greased her wheels, and she lived to be a hundred.

I once spent a night in an office-slash-garret on the fourth floor of Stalbridge Chambers. As a fling, it was nothing special, only...the image of my younger self perched on that window ledge, drinking from a wine-cask bladder at midnight, seems like a figure in a classical diorama: shadow melding with darker shadow, pinholes for stars. It would have been 1985, when hardly anyone actually lived in the CBD. The odd artist or millionaire-eccentric—that was about all. It felt illicit, and thrilling, to inhabit the nine-to-five city at night.

6:C

LITTLE QUEEN STREET (SYNAGOGUE LANE) → LITTLE BOURKE STREET

There was a time when Melburnians liked nothing better with their breakfast than a slum exposé in the paper. Under the guidance and protection of a police detective or municipal inspector of nuisances, some journalist would venture into his city's dankest, most crime-ridden quarters and report in juicy detail the abominations he witnessed there.

'Life there is like a hideous nightmare...a phantasmagoria

of horrors...' That was Marcus Clarke, writing in 1869, and *there* was Synagogue Lane. 'The record of our experiences in exploring its mysteries may be repulsive, but it is true':

> *Groups of women, mostly old and hideous, were standing at doorways, and saluted us with torrents of blasphemy and obscenity...The gutters were choked with filth, the walls blackened with slime...Children, whose faces more resembled those of monkeys than human beings, scrambled about in every variety of foulness. Infants, whose emaciated bodies were covered with running and evil-smelling sores, rolled among the heaps of rags and dirt that fronted the dwellings, while their mothers smoked, drank, and cursed on the doorsteps.*

Hard to picture now, isn't it?

The hovels of Synagogue Lane, like those of the Little Bourke 'back slums' generally, were nice little earners for their landlords who, if not parliamentarians or town councillors themselves, usually had friends who were. Once a journalist had lifted the rock, though, a process of sanitisation would begin—and often end—with a change of name. Thus Synagogue Lane became Bourke Lane. But the blight must have taken quite some shaking, since it ended up Little Queen Street.

Occupying one side of the lane was the eponymous synagogue, fronting Bourke Street with a Hebrew school behind. Land had been granted for the synagogue in 1844, though officials at the Colonial Office in London, when informed, opposed the grant as unlawful: only Christian faiths were eligible for government aid. But the sluggish pace of bureaucracy and mail ships meant that, by the time word of its illegitimacy reached Melbourne, the synagogue was already an established fact.

6:D

REDMOND BARRY'S COTTAGE

CORNER LITTLE BOURKE & THOMSON STREETS

Thomson Street used to be a dirt track—not even a lane—straggling inland through factory yards. At the far end was an old slate-roofed brick cottage that had once been Redmond Barry's house. In 1843—not yet Judge Barry, let alone Sir Redmond—he had it built well back from the street and surrounded it with garden. There were vegetables and grapevines in rows, as well as mulberry trees, leaves from which would supply feed for silkworms raised by Ann Timbrell of Northcote (the wife of a shorthand-writer), who, with encouragement from Barry and his colleagues in the Acclimatisation Society, tried establishing a local silk industry.

Barry hadn't long been living in the cottage when he met his life companion Louisa Barrow. But the pair would never have cohabited here. As his diary attests (in numeric detail) Barry preferred to dally with romantic partners at their own lodgings or even in the open air—anywhere but at his place. Once her husband was out of the picture, Barry set Mrs Barrow up in a house of her own (see 1:F) and would keep her in comfort, if at a distance, until his death in 1880.

By 1920, Barry's old cottage was used for storage by a second-hand dealer. Of the garden, just one bowed mulberry tree remained. Slates were slipping from the cottage roof and the paint-box windows had panes missing. But inside, still fixed to the wall in one room, was a tall cupboard with double doors. Its six shelves had once held Barry's personal library into which, a decade before he founded the Melbourne Public Library, he would invite respectable working men to dip for their edification. Some of the books from that cupboard are still in the State Library's collection, but the cupboard itself—like the cottage—is long gone.

Approaching Queen Street you'll notice Barry Lane, surely named for Sir Redmond. Or re-named. Before its AC/DC moment came, it was Tankards Lane—after Tankard's Temperance Hotel, which stood at the far end.

ST PATRICK'S HALL / FIRE TOWER

CORNER LITTLE BOURKE STREET & ST PATRICKS ALLEY

Next to the synagogue on Bourke Street was St Patrick's Hall, built in the 1840s for the St Patrick's Society, a social and charitable club for Melbourne's Irish-born. Before the gold rush it was the biggest hall in town, making it the natural choice for a temporary parliament house when Victoria first governed itself upon—*hallelujah!*—separation from New South Wales in 1851. From then on, the St Patrick's Society held two carnivals each year: one on St Patrick's Day (naturally), the other on the anniversary of separation.

When St Patrick's Hall was knocked down in 1957, Melburnians 'rediscovered' the old fire tower, behind it here on Little Bourke Street. Built in 1883 at Melbourne's highest point (seventy metres above sea level), the tower was itself almost the exact height (forty metres) that would later be set as the limit for city buildings. And elevation, of course, was the point of the fire tower: from a glassed-in room at the top, a spotter kept a look-out for untoward smoke—no easy matter in a city full of chimneys.

Fire was both power-source and scourge of the nineteenth-century city, what with all those steam engines and boilers, wood-fired stoves and ovens, open fireplaces, laundry coppers, oil lamps and candles, fireworks, bonfires, touchy matches and every man a smoker. With buildings close or conjoined and water in unsteady supply, even in Melbourne's broad streets (let alone the back lanes) a fire, once started, would spread like...you know what. And wooden buildings weren't the only worry; even those of brick and bluestone had timber floors and roof joists.

So the fire tower was, for a time, the tallest thing in the city. Surrounded by iron-framed glass and with a copper roof overhead, the spotter must have baked in summer. Occasionally, at shadowless noon, he might have company: a photographer capturing so-called 'balloon views' of the city. The tower commanded an uninterrupted panorama right out across the suburbs—except for a blind-spot to the west, thanks to the dome of the new law courts on William Street.* But with the tight-packed workers' terraces of West Melbourne a stronghold of labour politics, no doubt some in high places would have been happy to let 'em burn.

* In honour of the law courts, this slug of Little Bourke Street (between Queen and William) was, for about fifty years, known as Law Courts Place. The two blocks to the east were designated Post Office Place. Such particularising must have helped with wayfinding and perhaps also added prestige.

6:F

PASTORAL HOTEL RIOT

CORNER QUEEN & LITTLE BOURKE STREETS

Among the speakers at the first Melbourne meeting of the St Patrick's Society in 1842, one remarked:

> *Our poor unfortunate country has long been distracted by internal dissensions, political and religious; but we must now forget them all, and as colonizers of a new and lovely land, establish a character worthy the sons of the Emerald Isle.*

For many, though, no distance could blunt the force of sectarian feeling. In 1843, a local chapter of the Loyal Orange Order was formed, dedicated to the glory of the Protestant cause in Ireland. Their annual feast day commemorated the 1690 Battle of the Boyne, in which the victory of William III (William of Orange) overthrew Catholic rule in Ireland. To any Irish Catholic, the very name of the Orange Order was like a thumb in the eye.

The Pastoral Hotel, on this corner, was to be the venue of Melbourne's first Boyne anniversary dinner. From early on the appointed day Orange banners were flown from the upstairs windows and, by mid-afternoon, a crowd of maybe two hundred gathered in Queen Street 'to view the obnoxious banners'. One thing led to another: gunshots from the street met return fire from an upstairs window of the Pastoral Hotel. Two men in the street were shot (one of them intercepting a slug meant for the Catholic priest, Father Geoghegan, who was trying to disperse the crowd) and one in the bar of a hotel opposite. The Riot Act was read and soldiers stormed the Pastoral Hotel. Ringleaders were rounded up, and days of unrest followed. The *Argus* ran a highly partisan account of the 'Popish Riots', along with a call to arms titled 'The Protestant Warning', which began like this:

> *Ye Orangemen of Melbourne, who fondly dream'd the laws*
> *Were strong enough at least to clip the Papist rabble's claws,*
> *No longer on the broken reed of Government rely,*
> *But 'put your trust in God, my Boys, and keep your powder dry!'*

To defuse the situation, the authorities ended up dropping all charges, but within months an Act would outlaw the carrying of weapons in connection with any religious or political gathering, or of banners 'calculated to provoke animosity'.

The Orangemen found a way around the ban in 1867, when their contribution to the 'illuminations' welcoming Prince Alfred, the Duke of Edinburgh, to Melbourne (see 5:E) was a transparency on the front of Protestant Hall in

Stephen Street, featuring William III crossing the River Boyne and the words *This We Will Maintain*. Riled-up Catholics turned out in force the first night the transparency was lit, to throw stones and sing 'The Wearing of the Green'. Shots fired from an upstairs window this time killed a fifteen-year-old in the street. 'If the obnoxious exhibition had been removed in time,' concluded the coroner, 'the crime of murder would not have been committed.'

6:G

MUSEUM OF BUILDING MATERIALS

CORNER QUEEN & LITTLE LONSDALE STREETS

The first stage of Parliament House was built of sombre bluestone and plebeian brick, in the knowledge that at the next stage it would be hidden by more genteel materials. But they proved hard to find (see 3:S). A government Building Stone Commission in 1858 offered a reward to the discoverer of local stone good enough for Parliament House. Only half the reward money was paid, however, for a 'very fair' stone—from Darley, near Bacchus Marsh—which would have to do 'until a better one is discovered'.

The head of the commission was J. G. Knight, the son of a building stone merchant in London who'd trained as an architect before joining the gold rush in 1852. Now he was overseeing the construction of Parliament House, having contributed to its design.* It was in light of the building-stone dilemma that Knight came up with the idea for a Museum of Building Materials, which took shape on this spot in 1859. And a pretty strange shape it was.

It wasn't a museum in the usual sense: the building itself was the exhibit. One side wall was supported by pillars of stone—each pillar of a different kind—separated by panels of brickwork exemplifying varieties not only of brick, but of mortar as well. On the other side of the building the order was reversed, with pillars of brick and panels of stone. Blocks of different granites made up the rear wall, while the foundation level all round was of bluestone dressed in a variety of styles. Out front, the stuccoed façade was riotous with ornamental scrolls, pedestals and entablatures, and a patchwork of slates, terracotta tiles, galvanised iron, zinc, copper and wooden shingles made up the roof. Even the fencing was experimental, with no two posts the same: various timbers were used—some tarred, some charred—to see which best withstood decay. Adding to the building's oddity, every material and decorative element was labelled. By one report, 'It looked as if it had been put up by a very mad architect.'

The 'ingenious' and 'indefatigable' J. G. Knight expected it would take years for the museum to prove its

* Others of Knight's buildings still standing in the CBD include the Sam Yup Society 'courthouse' in Little Bourke Street (see 3:G) and the Mickveh Yisrael synagogue and school in Exhibition Street (4:F).

worth fully, allowing time for the weathering process to take effect on the promiscuous elements, and with new materials added or substituted as they became available. In the meantime, builders and architects could treat the building as a catalogue of materials and styles, referring in their contracts to such-and-such a sample on view at the museum.

There was talk of exhibiting art in the building's sky-lit main hall, as 'the first step towards a future National Gallery'. But even before it was completed, the government had lost interest in the museum ('that expensive toy') and refused to spend any more money on it. Few Melburnians—let alone visitors—ever knew the purpose of the curious hodge-podge on Queen Street. Politicians mocked it as 'a farce' and 'a cross between a child's playhouse and a Chinese Pagoda', and likened its experimental function to 'selecting one straw from a haystack and giving it to a jackass to eat, as a test of the remainder of the stack'. In London, though, it was hailed as visionary and inspired a similar venture that would eventually form part of the Victoria and Albert Museum.

In 1860, Melbourne's Museum of Building Materials became the office of the new Department of Mines, being 'of no earthly use to anybody else'. From the outset, though, the clerks and geologists complained that it was 'injudicious to have the windows in the roof'. Sun poured in and so did rain. (J. G. Knight pointed out the building was 'never designed to stand sound and intact'.) After just fifteen years, Knight's folly was slated for demolition, in disregard of any insights its leaky, crumbling fabric might offer. Which was a pity because, as one writer reflected in 1875:

> *Opinion is yet a good deal divided on the question of whether we have any durable building stone in Victoria. A good many structures in which Victorian stone has been used represent a chronic condition of exfoliation, so that architects and builders together have persuaded most people to put up their houses of brick, and to smear them with that most villainous of shams, stucco.*

Sure enough, the palatial offices of the Registrar-General, replacing the Museum of Building Materials, were built not of stone but of stucco-smeared brick.

Diagonally opposite, at the north-east corner of Queen and Little Lonsdale, stands a townhouse that originally belonged to publican, theatre-owner and Melbourne mayor J. T. Smith. Built in stages from around 1850, it was leased by the government in 1858 as overflow storage for gold that wouldn't fit in their own treasury vault. (See 6:J.)

6:H

WOMEN'S VD CLINIC

372–8 LITTLE LONSDALE STREET

Venereal disease spiked with the return of soldiers from active service in World War One. In Melbourne more than 6,500 cases, about a fifth of them women, were treated in 1917–18 for what was dubbed 'the Red Plague'. A men's VD clinic was set up in Lonsdale Street in 1918, with this red-brick edifice built the following year as a clinic for women. It ran in conjunction with the Queen Victoria Hospital for Women and Children, then in its original home, practically opposite at the corner of Little Lonsdale and William streets.

In the pre-penicillin age, venereal diseases could be hard to shake. Children born with syphilis had their lives cut short by it, while hucksters grew rich peddling quack cures for 'youthful indiscretions'. Treatments, some containing mercury, were about as likely to kill as to cure. Such was the crisis during and after the First World War that laws were passed, in Europe, America and Australia, to make notification and treatment of VD mandatory. In 1916, Dr Harriet Clisby (see 5:B and 6:B) wrote in support of such a law: 'It has never been found possible to protect the community from the ravages of infectious and contagious diseases by educative means alone: compulsion has always been necessary.'

The plan was that, following treatment at this clinic, women would be detained at a sanatorium in the suburbs 'until the risk of infection has passed'. The government bought a mansion by the river at Kew for the purpose, but local residents objected. While the search for an acceptable site continued, recuperating women were confined in the prison hospital at Pentridge.

The location in Little Lonsdale Street of the women's VD clinic linked it, in the public imagination, with Little Lon, five blocks to the east. (See 4:B and 4:C.) In vain did the authorities insist that 'some' sufferers 'are of a quite unblameworthy type'. In 1925, a government enquiry into the effects of alcohol on health—inspired by the American experiment with prohibition—heard from one expert, Dr Joseph Love, that consumption of alcohol was implicated in a third of venereal disease cases in women, with those who frequented wine shops being the most at risk. 'Wine is the devil in their fate,' said Dr Love.

When planning was underway for the new building that looms overhead, heritage activists fought to save the old VD clinic and its neighbour, a former tuberculosis clinic. It had been decades since either served its original function, but still (it was claimed) 'they speak wonderfully about so many aspects of our city's history'. In a gesture condemned as 'façadism', only their frontages have been kept as streetscape features. Me, I don't mind a façade: it keeps things interesting at street level.

After the Royal Mint was built facing William Street in 1870, this flanking section of Little Lonsdale Street was denominated Mint Place. The name doesn't seem to have stuck for long. Probably the infectious disease clinics took the shine off it.

OLD EXHIBITION BUILDING

CORNER WILLIAM & LITTLE LONSDALE STREETS

Before the Mint supplanted it, Melbourne's original exhibition building stood here. Built in 1854 for the city's first exhibition of industries and arts, it was an ungainly and impractical structure: a two-storey framework of timber and iron, painted white, inset with two hundred long windows and roofed mainly in glass. Hot and leaky, it was affectionately known as the Melon Frame.

That first exhibition was a pallid affair compared to the extravaganzas of later decades. Most of the exhibits were connected with agriculture or goldmining, and there were more imported goods than local ones on display. One striking demonstration of industry and culture in action, though, was the printing press of the *Age* which produced the newspaper's first issue on the spot.

There would be a couple more exhibitions held here, including the city's first fine arts show, curated in 1858 by J. G. Knight (see 6:G). He would also stage-manage the 1861 exhibition here, previewing Victorian exhibits bound for the next year's London International Exhibition. The showstopper was of Knight's own invention: a massive gilded pyramid representing all the gold mined in the colony to that date. (It went on to win a prize in London.)

For years, the exhibition building was a much-used—if complained-of—public utility, hosting bazaars, civil service exams, political rallies, even the very first classes of the University of Melbourne. And, being spacious and lit by three hundred gas-lamps, it was an ideal venue for evening entertainments: concerts and, especially, balls.

The ball of the Patriotic Fund (aiding the British war effort in the Crimea) was held there in July 1855 and acclaimed as 'the most brilliant ever given in the colony'. The cloakroom arrangements also set a benchmark: 'Such a scene of confusion we believe never occurred as the sequel to any similar entertainment.' It seems the attendants abandoned their posts around two in the morning after several gentlemen stormed the cloakroom and, in disregard of the ticketing system, insisted on retrieving their own hats and coats. All over town next day, 'people were to be met who, by the novel fit of their chapeau, showed that they had been at the ball and had suffered from the chaos of the cloak-room'.

A flurry of notices in the 'Lost or Found' columns of the press sought the return of garments 'taken in error' on the night of the ball:

> *The Gentleman who took a Top Coat (brown colour), with a Silk Handkerchief with red border, and some Cigars in the pockets, is requested to return it...*
>
> *Lost at the Exhibition Building, a Dark Blue Cloth Poncho, having a pair of India-rubber Galoshes, Kid Gloves, and a white Wideawake Hat in the lower pockets...*

In what may be a clue to the real cause of the cloakroom cock-up, the drinking of spirits was pointedly banned at the next ball to be held in the exhibition building. Also, the cloakroom entrance was barricaded after midnight, with the desired result: 'the utmost order prevailed'.

Within just a few years, it was commonplace to read of 'the crazy old Exhibition Building'. The timber framework was warping, panes of glass cracking. In summer, the glare and heat made it practically unusable. Canvas was fitted over the glass roof to keep out sun and rain. True, in 1866 it gave welcome shelter to some four hundred castaways from the ship *Netherby*, wrecked near King Island. But when Melbourne's first Intercolonial Exhibition was mooted for 1867 there was no question of staging it in 'such a rickety old structure'. Instead, for that occasion, a new exhibition hall was built behind the Public Library.

Residents of West Melbourne wanted to turn the old exhibition building into a local market. But no go. (The Queen Victoria Market was still ten years off.) By 1868, the Melon Frame was reduced to a target (or 'cockshy') for stones thrown by boys and, figuratively, by the Melbourne press, which deplored that 'this valuable plateau...the most commanding site for a public building in the western part of the city' should be occupied by such an eyesore. In 1869, the site was claimed for the Melbourne branch of the Royal Mint and the old exhibition building was sold as scrap, with the half-comic suggestion that it might be resurrected at the botanic gardens as a hothouse.

As a Prussian army officer, Gustav Techow was guarding the Berlin arsenal when it was stormed by insurgents in 1848. Not only did he willingly hand out arms, he joined the uprising. When it was crushed, Techow fled to Switzerland and was tried and sentenced, in absentia, for treason. He remained active in revolutionary circles and his writings influenced Marx and Engels, whose *Communist Manifesto* had been published in 1848. On meeting Marx, Techow marked his 'outstanding intellectual superiority' and 'most impressive personality': 'If he had as much heart as brain, as much love as hate, I would have gone through fire with him.' But Techow left 'convinced that everything good in him has been devoured by the most dangerous personal ambitions'. Even so, the pair would keep in touch long after Techow joined the surge of gold-seekers to Melbourne in 1852.

In time, he'd be appointed head of the National Gymnasium, instructing school teachers in military drill and gymnastics. Outfitted for the purpose was a lofty corrugated iron coach-shed behind the exhibition building. When the site was cleared for the Mint, the gymnasium shed, with Techow in charge, was relocated to Jolimont where it would nestle beside the Melbourne Cricket Ground until 1906.

6:J

OLD OLD TREASURY

CORNER WILLIAM & LONSDALE STREETS

In gold-rush times, most of Melbourne officialdom was quartered in and around William Street. Diagonally opposite here, where the law courts now stand, was the office of the governor, in those days Victoria's head of government. In Lonsdale Street itself was the government printing office and in La Trobe Street, near William, were the offices of the Lands Department, responsible for the all-important sale and lease of Crown* lands as well as the initial management of the goldfields. And on this corner a three-storey bluestone building housed the Survey Department upstairs and on the ground floor, the Treasury.

Gold brought down to Melbourne by government escort during the early months of the gold rush in 1851 was stored in the vaults of the city's handful of banks. So heavy was the golden harvest, though, that the bank vaults were soon full and a strongroom had to be added to the rear of the Treasury office. When its first consignment from Mount Alexander (Castlemaine) arrived one afternoon in January 1852, the clerks and draughtsmen in the upper offices crowded at the windows, boggle-eyed at the sight of three drays weighed down with other men's gold. A run of resignations followed, as many among the survey staff opted to try *their* luck at the diggings.

Over the next five years, more than six million ounces of gold passed through the treasury—and some of it never left there. Parcels of gold would go unclaimed if, for instance, a digger died, or if he lost the receipt issued when he deposited it. Treasury clerks (much in the manner of election officials in the American south) would demand proof of identity and even ask a digger to describe his particular parcel of gold—which was tricky, since most were sent in plain chamois bags. Should he fail to satisfy the official,

* The British crown's ownership of the whole of Melbourne and the Port Phillip district was firmly asserted when Batman's 1835 'treaty' with the land's traditional owners was disallowed.

his gold would be withheld, falling into 'the convenient whirlpool of the general revenue'. Eventually, the Treasury strongroom's capacity would be so over-stretched that the cellar of a nearby townhouse had to be co-opted as supplementary gold-storage. (See 6:G) It was mainly to centralise and secure the government gold-vaults that a substantial new treasury (now the Old Treasury) was built in Spring Street in 1859. After that, the building on this corner (call it the old, old treasury) was for years a hotel and boarding house, then sung into extinction by the customary headline: *Historic landmark disappearing.*

6:K

JESSIE DUNN'S HOUSE

523 LITTLE LONSDALE STREET (CORNER WICKLOW LANE)

> *The growing good of the world is partly dependent on unhistoric acts; and that things are not so ill with you and me as they might have been, is half owing to the number who lived faithfully a hidden life, and rest in unvisited tombs.*
>
> George Eliot, *Middlemarch*

Here, for twenty-one of her twenty-two years, lived Jessie Dunn—a nobody. Born in 1857, she was the only child of Louisa and Robert Dunn. Her grandfather, Thomas Odell, was minister of the Congregational Church on Lonsdale Street, close by, and a man of puritanical bent. His daughter, Jessie's mother, was a stalwart of the Ladies' Benevolent Society. Jessie's father worked at the Customs House as a shipping registrar. As for Jessie herself, she was a dutiful Victorian daughter.

At seventeen, she was courted by the brother of a school-friend living in La Trobe Street. They took walks together on Flagstaff Hill and attended the Intercolonial Exhibition of 1875, staged in the hall behind the Public Library. They seemed to be growing close, and then…she ended it. Her parents disapproved, Jessie told her sweetheart, and she could not disobey their wishes. Was it because he questioned the existence of heaven and hell? Or because she had tuberculosis? Did she even know?

Spurned, the young man left Melbourne forever. Only when Jessie died, four years later, did he learn of her illness. But that wasn't the end of Jessie—not for him, anyway. Now living in Boston and making his name as an investigator of 'psychical' phenomena, he communicated with Jessie in séances, elevating their love to a pitch it never reached in life. And when, after his own death, decades later, he re-established contact with the living via his favourite medium, they'd ask about Jessie and he would reply, 'She is with me now.'

Jessie Dunn was nowhere but she was everywhere.

KILKENNY INN

CORNER LONSDALE & KING STREETS → VIA HEALEY LANE

A public meeting at Martin Healey's Kilkenny Inn, on this corner, in the winter of 1853 called for action on the impassable state of King Street. Being 'in the direct line from the wharves to the gold-diggings', this was one of the city's most important arteries. For carters of supplies to the goldfields, King Street was a mere taste of what lay ahead: bogs alternating with boulders and unbridged creek crossings.

To be honest, I've avoided this intersection for years. With strip clubs on two corners it's felt like hostile territory: Loserville.

The Reverend Thomas Odell's church stood just a few doors from here, on Lonsdale Street. If, like his granddaughter, Odell kept abreast of doings in this wicked world after he left it, how his vestigial sensibilities must be flayed by the turn his neighbourhood has taken. In life, he deplored the *theatre* as a malign influence on 'the proper rules of morality'—what would he have made of Goldfingers and the Men's Gallery? Perhaps it's the censorious spirit of Reverend Odell that infuses me whenever I pass this way. But I doubt it.

6:M

MCCUBBIN'S BAKERY
165 KING STREET

Frederick McCubbin, acclaimed artist of the Heidelberg School, was born in his parents' King Street bakery, on this spot, in 1855. He attended the West Melbourne Common School, close by, and all his mates were King Street boys. One of them, Louis Brennan, lived opposite the McCubbins in a bluestone cottage and would find fame during World War I as inventor of the steerable torpedo.

After his elder brother, Jim, went to sea, young Fred McCubbin became a delivery boy, carting bread all over town and to the docks. He then apprenticed to a King Street wheelwright, until a fancy-painted dray inspired him to learn drawing. Studying art at night, he worked by day for Stevenson & Elliott, King Street coachbuilders, giving decorative paint jobs to drays and carts and coaches. Several of McCubbin's early paintings depict his King Street milieu: the family kitchen, old George Elliott (the coachbuilder looking sage in a painting titled *An Old Politician*), and *Girl with Bird at the King Street Bakery*, his last painting before he turned to the bush scenes for which he's best known. *Girl with Bird* gives the view through the bakery's back gate from Uniacke Court. The girl wears a pinafore, the bird's a magpie, pecking at crumbs.

Fred McCubbin left King Street in 1889, but would return in the 1900s as a weekday lodger at the Rose of Australia Hotel (at the corner of King and Bourke), where his sisters were landladies. Brother Jim died far from his old home when the *Lusitania*, of which he was chief purser, was hit by a German torpedo in 1915.

6:N

WESTWARD

CORNER LITTLE BOURKE STREET & PENDER ALLEY

If you think the prose employed in real-estate listings today is overheated, consider the adverts placed by property agents selling the parcel of land between Uniacke Court and Pender Alley in 1888. Sales notices for 'this magnificent block of land…situated in the most rising position in the city' trumpeted the 'Broad Carriage Ways and Light on Three Sides' before degenerating into *verse*:

> *Westward the tide of empires rolls its way,*
> *So will this grand metropolis,*
> *Westward the tide of business rolls,*
> *Westward the tide of increase rolls.*

'In fact,' concluded the sales pitch, in case you'd somehow missed the point, 'the tidal wave of prosperity is westward.'

The west owed its pulling power to the epic Spencer Street railway goods shed (see 2:Q), then under construction.

Fifty-one years later, a bag of gold bullion sent by mail train from Bendigo went missing in the short distance between Spencer Street station and the mail sorting depot opposite. The empty canvas bag, its mail seals cut off, was later found in Pender Alley. It smelled of an inside job, but the culprit(s) got clean away with the gold.

6:O

LAST OF THE LITTLE BOURKE LANES

ROSE ALLEY & LANGS LANE

We've sampled laneways the full length of Little Bourke Street. These two, the last of them, are typical in that a shallow dip into the old newspapers brings up stories of utter misery and degradation within their narrow confines. Granted, newspapers tend to trade in the sensational, distorting the reality of most people going peaceably about their business (all those 'hidden lives'). Still, it's worth noting the legacy of violence that clings to the city's laneways. It was an everyday thing to read of a woman being killed—or close to it—in yards or dwellings down lanes and alleys like these. Usually her assailant was the man she lived with and almost always there was alcohol involved.

Jane Irwin was beaten and kicked to death by her 'paramour' in a 'wretched house' in Rose Alley. As always, at the inquest, plenty of neighbours came forward to tell what they'd seen and heard. ('Oh Ned, don't choke me.')

Joanna Murphy's husband, 'in a mad drunken state', sliced off her nose while she dozed outside her doorway in Langs Lane. Accusing her of 'whoredom', his only regret was that he hadn't cut her throat.

And on it goes. Up any laneway, bodies bob to the surface. Not just women's, it's true: men frequently met with violence in the laneways, only less often in their homes. You read too of children brutalised by beatings and neglect, sometimes resulting in their deaths. And with contraception all but non-existent and abortion illegal, infanticide was no rare thing. In Langs Lane, a newborn wrapped in newspaper was the eighth infant found dead in Melbourne in the first six weeks of 1905. 'Child Murder Seems to be Rampant' ran the *Herald*'s headline.

In the 1986 heist comedy *Malcolm*, the plucky heroes (played by Colin Friels and John Hargreaves) shook off their police pursuers by darting up Langs Lane from Bourke Street, each piloting half of a lengthwise-bisected yellow Honda Z (a 1970s micro-hatch). What made it such a feat is that Langs Lane, where it joins Bourke Street, is barely two shoulders wide.*

* Only Corrs Lane (see 3:J) is skinnier.

6:P

HUDSON'S STORES

655 BOURKE STREET

When the camera swung round to show the thwarted rozzers in that getaway scene from *Malcolm*, visible behind them was Hudson's Stores, on this spot. Hudson's had sold hardware there since the 1920s but, by the time I knew it, sixty years later, its window display was full of military surplus gear, all grimy and moth-eaten. It shared with the Job Warehouse (see 3:P), at Bourke Street's other end, a curmudgeonly style of commerce. Each was run by a pair of brothers disinclined to waste time on customers who didn't know exactly what they were looking for. Browsers never got to see the good stuff.

Not being a seamstress, I wasn't much tempted to penetrate the Job Warehouse stronghold. But in the window of Hudson's was a square-necked sailor's shirt and detachable flap collar, so alluring (to me) that I summoned the courage to enter. Inside, all was gloomy-dark and unkempt and smelling of engine oil. Among piles of surplus, I found the sailors' shirts as well as a navy uniform dress skirt. Was there a change room? The gruff fellow at the counter pointed to a glassed-in office whose windows were pasted over with sheets of newspaper, only peeled away in places to put the kybosh on privacy. After a hasty try-on, I bought the outfit, along with a scary-looking (in a good way) leather ammo belt.

Hudson's Stores left Bourke Street in 1987. Of my Hudson's purchase, I still have the collar, navy blue with white piping. It's supposed to be lucky to *touch* a sailor's collar. How lucky does that make me?

6:Q

AFTERMATH OF THE LETTSOM RAID

CORNER BOURKE & KING STREETS

The land now bounded by Spencer, Bourke, King and Collins streets was reserved in Melbourne's first year of existence as the settlement's government precinct. Originally covered with 'verdure green as a leek and soft as a Turkey carpet', the reserve soon was peppered with an assortment of unpretentious and, mostly, makeshift structures. Among them were police station, lock-up and various colonial government offices, outposts of their 'parent' instrumentalities in Sydney.

On this spot, in 1840, was built a brick storehouse roughly five metres square, with barred windows and a roof of wooden shingles. It was meant for use by the Commissariat Department next door and was still unfinished when, that October, it was recruited as a makeshift cell for between one and two hundred Indigenous people—many of them women and children—who'd been rounded up in an early morning raid on their camp at Merri Creek.

The settlement of Melbourne had led to settlement of the wider Port Phillip District, mostly as squatters' sheep runs. Almost overnight, the land and waterways became contested property, with Indigenous people treated as intruders and denied access to their country, its resources and sacred places. Troops of Border Police* sent from Sydney were authorised to deal harshly with 'incursions' onto squatters' land and 'threats' to their persons or property. In 1840, three shepherds were killed in the Goulburn River district (north-east of Melbourne) and a troop headed by a Major Lettsom was charged with tracking down the culprits, said to be Taungurong men. Lettsom searched in vain and had retreated to Melbourne when he learned that his suspects were among a large gathering of Taungurong and local (Woiwurrung and Boonwurrung) people camped not far from town. Reinforced with police and soldiers, Lettsom and his men descended on the camp at dawn with weapons drawn. A young Taungurong man named Winberri, 'a noted ringleader', was shot and killed when he confronted the raiders with his waddy raised. (One of the government-appointed 'protectors', who'd met Winberri on country, would remember him as a 'noble

* The borders they policed were the frontiers between so-called 'settled areas' (mainly, the squatters' vast leaseholdings) and the diminishing rest (deemed 'unalienated' land).

minded' man who'd saved the lives of shepherds and travellers in the bush.)

As many as three hundred people ('the remainder of the gang') were rounded up at the Merri Creek campsite and 'escorted' at bayonet-point to town, where they were herded into a fenced yard on the government reserve. Any settler with an axe to grind was invited to identify 'troublemakers' among them. Particularly 'conspicuous and busy' was squatter Peter Snodgrass who pointed the finger at many of the thirty-five 'ruffians' singled out and gaoled. Of those remaining, any recognised as 'Melbourne blacks' were let go, with the rest crammed into the unfinished brick storehouse on this spot, pending further identification.

The building didn't yet have a door, so boards were nailed across the doorway and two sentries posted outside. Around two in the morning, a neighbour awoke to find the captives streaming out through a hole burrowed under the building's back wall. He sounded the alarm and some of the inmates made a rush at the barred doorway. One, a man named Wo-ondeek, was killed by a soldier's bullet. The few terrified prisoners remaining—mostly women, some with children—were released 'with small rations' the next morning.

In the aftermath of the raid George Robinson, head of the Port Phillip Aboriginal Protectorate, visited the campsite on the Clifton Hill side of Merri Creek, where 'The natives' utensils lay scattered about in every possible direction spears, broken rope and different articles of clothing…'

'Malicious and evil disposed white persons' looted the campsite then set it alight, shooting 'a vast number' of dogs. The raid itself Robinson condemned not just as 'harsh and heart-rending', but as an 'illegal proceeding'.

Two of the three Melbourne newspapers likewise deplored as 'woeful' the raid and what followed. Official enquiries were mounted, with the eventual result that Governor Gipps, in Sydney, was mildly castigated by his superiors at the Colonial Office in London. Long before that, though, the thirty-five men in custody were subjected to 'repeated examinations', after which only ten were detained, charged with armed robbery—of flour and mutton—from a shepherd's hut on Snodgrass's run near Yea. They were said to have been led by Winberri who, reasoning that 'the sheep eat the grass belonging to his kangaroo, and white fellow took kangaroo', demanded a *quid pro quo*.

At their trial, in January 1841, nine of the ten men were convicted—in spite of 'a forcible and eloquent speech' in their defence by Redmond Barry*—and sentenced to ten years' transportation on Norfolk Island. With other prisoners, they were put on a boat, under military guard, to rendezvous in the bay with a ship bound for Sydney. Where the Yarra (on its original course) narrowed near its junction with the Maribyrnong River, the Taungurong

* The only newspaper to mention it regretted that 'we had it not in our power to give a correct report' of Barry's speech, there being no shorthand writer on staff—or in Melbourne.

men, all wearing leg-irons, leapt overboard and made for shore. Two or more were shot, presumed killed; another, Tarrak-munnin, was hauled aboard with bullet wounds; the rest got away. At least, the *Port Phillip Patriot* hoped so: 'better that six felons should escape than that the guilt of so much human blood, spilt through mismanagement (to use the mildest term), should rest with the authorities here'.

A few months later, a new use was found for the brick storehouse on this spot. Now fitted with a door, it became the town's first Supreme Court. Up till then, Melbourne had no judge, just a handful of magistrates, and anyone charged with a serious crime had to be sent to Sydney for trial.

But hang on—hadn't the Taungurong men been charged with armed robbery? Indeed—and since Melbourne's Quarter Sessions court had lacked the authority to try them, it turned out their convictions were illegal. Not only that, but La Trobe (not yet governor, but superintendent of the Port Phillip District) had reviewed the men's case and concluded there wasn't 'one tittle of evidence' against them.

So when Judge Willis convened the Supreme Court in May, one of his first acts was to pardon the nine Taungurong men, of whom only Tarrak-munnin remained in custody. In fact the *Patriot*, which had fostered hopes for the escapees, now believed Tarrak-munnin to be the sole survivor, and reflected with 'horror' on 'such a wanton waste of human life'.

Speaking of which, it was in the little brick courthouse on this corner that, seven months later, Judge Willis would sentence Tunnaminnerwait and Maulboyheenner to death by hanging. (See 4:L.)

WALK 7

OFF THE GRID

In which we explore the city's northern outskirts by go-cart

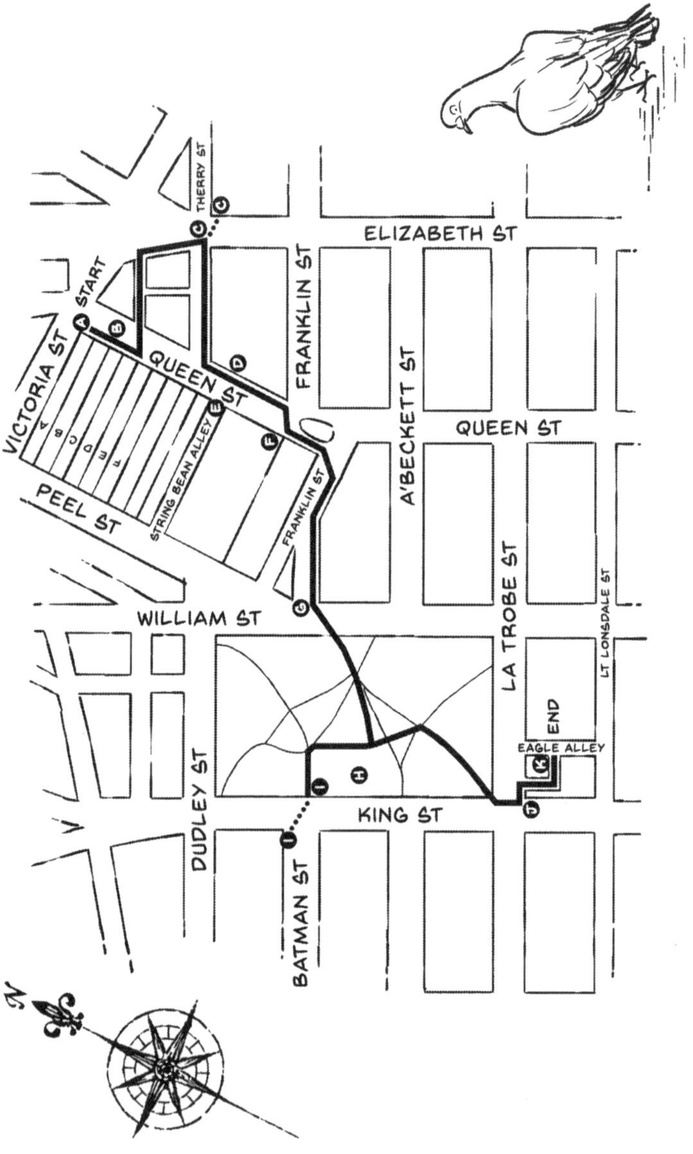

START
VICTORIA ST
QUEEN ST
PEEL ST
STRING BEAN ALLEY
FRANKLIN ST
THERRY ST
ELIZABETH ST
A'BECKETT ST
QUEEN ST
LA TROBE ST
LT LONSDALE ST
WILLIAM ST
DUDLEY ST
KING ST
BATMAN ST
EAGLE ALLEY
END
N

7:A

UBIQUITOUS VICTORIA
CORNER VICTORIA & QUEEN STREETS

Here we are: the Queen Victoria Market, and the junction of Queen and Victoria streets. There was a broken-record quality to civic naming conventions during the long reign of the blessed Queen, from 1837 to 1901.* Especially here, in the capital of...Victoria.

> *In no part of the British Empire is more loyal and devoted attachment entertained towards the throne and person of our most gracious sovereign than in this city, the capital of the colony which is honoured with Her Majesty's name.*
> (Address by the mayor of Melbourne, 1881)

Was it abject toadyism, like that time when Tony Abbott conferred a knighthood on Prince Philip? No, the adoration was mostly for real. Royalty, back then, was the apex of celebrity, the monarch like a god you could put a face to. And so...Victoria.

When plans to separate the Port Phillip District from New South Wales were being hammered out in Whitehall in 1847, the name proposed for the new colony was Victoria.

* 'Victoria' still ranks ninth among Australia's most common street names.

The Melbourne press conceded it was 'a very pretty name, a right royal one' but worried that, given the proliferation of places bearing the same imperial mark of favour, it was 'a very indifferent *distinguishing* name'. Within just a few years, the names of Victoria's goldfields—Ballarat, Bendigo, Mount Alexander—would be household words in even the remotest corners of the British Isles. Yet still, in 1862, the *Argus* could gripe that the colony of Victoria itself was 'less known than Cariboo or Abeokuta', merged ignominiously under the umbrella term 'Australia'.* This meant, of course, that the other colonies got credit for *our* glorious achievements:

> *Almost the youngest, we claim to be the most vigorous of England's off-shoots. In proportion to our population, we are by far the richest community in the world, and by far the best customer that England has among the nations. Among the colonies we are the least burdensome of all to the mother country. Melbourne, our capital, has the metropolitan character in a marked degree, and is more like London, perhaps, than any city out of England. Compared to her, Sydney and Adelaide and Hobart Town are small and rather dull provincial towns.*

Yet 'we are systematically neglected and passed over by the

* Letters from abroad would be addressed to 'Melbourne, South Australia' (which was geographically correct) or, worse, 'Melbourne, New South Wales'.

mother country', and the writer for the *Argus* reckoned he knew why. The 'egregious bad taste, or flunkeyism' of the colony's framers had made Victoria 'the Smith among nations'. Swallowed up by the mass of Victorias, our particular greatness went unnoticed.

It was a good story anyway.

The streets of Melbourne's main grid had been named (just) before Victoria was crowned.* Perhaps if they hadn't been—if, say, Collins Street had been made Victoria Street instead—the colony itself would have got a more distinctive name. As it was, Victoria Street, marking the long northern boundary of Hoddle's 1837 survey, was named later than the rest.

The thing to notice is that Victoria Street defies the grid. Melbourne, to this point, lies on a grid angled northeast–southwest, an orientation determined by the course of the Yarra. But the surveyor's boundary, respecting only the compass, set things straight: Victoria Street runs east–west. The market sheds, running back in bays along Queen Street, follow the angle of Victoria Street. And Queen Street itself changes course where it borders the market, breaking with the grid to run north–south.

* Queen Street was named for the consort of William IV, whose death in 1837 brought Victoria to the throne.

7:B

OLD CEMETERY

QUEEN VIC MARKET SHEDS A–F

Perhaps another reason the market follows compass lines rather than the city grid is that this used to be the site of Melbourne's cemetery. By tradition, Christian burials were aligned feet to the east, head to the west (to face the second coming).

This was the town's main cemetery only from 1839 to 1853 (although interments in family plots continued here into the twentieth century). The ground nearest Victoria Street, unconsecrated, was set aside for Aborigines and suicides, and this was the part of the cemetery uprooted in 1878 to make way for the sheds of the new market.

In its eagerness to get everyone on board with the plan to relocate the wholesale vegetable market from its overcrowded site in Bourke Street East, the Melbourne city council claimed that the new market would occupy only that portion of the cemetery that was 'unused'. They should have added '…as far as we can tell'. Burials there were unmarked, discoverable only by digging, and before any market sheds were built the graves of twenty-eight 'all but unknown persons' would be exhumed and re-interred at the then-new cemetery in Carlton. These included Maulboyheenner and Tunnaminnerwait, from the Indigenous section marked out only three days before their execution (see 4:B), as well as a Quaker buried there 'by mistake'. At the far end of market sheds D, E and F, several Jewish graves were allowed to remain, and they would become part of a chicken-yard before being removed—over protests—when the sheds were eventually extended.

Along the back of F Shed runs a red-brick wall inlaid with arches of a lighter (originally white) brick, which marks the limit of the original market sheds. In 1878 it was deemed 'objectionable only to have an open iron railing between a busy market and a resting place for the dead'. But those archways…Though they were filled in from the start with solid brick, they seem to hint that the barrier between dead and living is a permeable one.

During the 1920s and '30s the market would expand to take over the old cemetery in its entirety, displacing and erasing as many as ten thousand pioneer graves. Of those, only 914 were decorously relocated, meaning a great many human remains were either left behind or carted away with the topsoil.* (Residents of nearby Parkville, finding human bones in soil dumped there, complained of the 'repulsive graveyard smell'.) Though the cemetery had long been overgrown and neglected (all those 'unvisited tombs'), churchmen and historians deplored its desecration and Jonah, a newspaper poet, composed an elegy:

* Many, perhaps most, graves were unmarked, the old wooden headstones having long ago been taken for firewood.

The car-bell tolls. 'Tis morn of market day,
And hordes of homely housewives baskets bear;
Their words of weal and woe, in woman's way,
Make trembling music in the ambient air.
'God's acre, please!' The clanging car is stayed,
Go-carts unfold, perambulators pass,
Converging where our pioneers were laid
Beneath the kindly covert of the grass.
The rude forefathers of the hamlet hear
Above their heads the call of 'Cabbagee!'
While onions provoke the silent tear,
And beetroots blush for frail mortality.

7:C

STORK HOTEL

CORNER ELIZABETH & THERRY STREETS

The Stork Hotel, which stood on the corner diagonally opposite until 2013, began as a landmark watering hole for travellers heading out of town or back again. In the 1850s the city council's cattle yards and hay market, which preceded the Vic Market on this side of the street, would invariably be described as 'opposite the Stork Hotel'. The odd-shaped parcel of land between Therry and Victoria streets wasn't put to a permanent use until 1868 when the council built its meat market there.

Elizabeth Street along here was scoured out by run-off that streamed downhill from the north and west, with gutters so deep they needed footbridges for crossing.* When the drainage was piped underground in the 1880s the street just here was slightly realigned, adding a narrow triangle of land to the front of the market, on which was built this row of two-storey shops. At the same time, the meat market—at the Victoria Street corner—got its ornamental façade, counterpointing beatific farm animals with ram skulls. (Think of it as truth in advertising.)

In the 2000s, the Stork Hotel was best known for its brainfood. It staged readings of Greek and Roman epics and theatrical adaptations of works by Proust, Camus and Duras, and served up moral dilemmas at regular Socratic dinners. In its early years, the Stork had hosted meetings of local ironworkers agitating for an eight-hour working day and of the Saltwater (i.e. Maribyrnong) River Protection Society, protesting the 'objectionable' practice of netting. A shortlived outfit calling itself the Amateur Benevolent Comedian Club met at the Stork to plan benefit performances for causes like the Burke and Wills monument and a memorial to Ellen Mortyn, a popular comic actress who died of TB.†

* Remember, Elizabeth Street followed the course of a natural gully draining into the Yarra. (See 2:D.)

† Mortyn's reputation was posthumously sullied by rumours that she'd died from complications of an abortion performed by Dr L. L. Smith (see 3:U). An inquest found otherwise.

Acquired for redevelopment, the Stork Hotel closed in 2007 after 150 years' trading and, following its demolition, the site was subjected to a post-mortem archaeological dig. (Not that the cause of death was any mystery.) In among the bluestone foundations were found bottles, coins and crockery fragments—pretty much what you'd expect. But also, in keeping with evidence seen elsewhere of Melbourne's shifting street levels, archaeologists found that this part of Elizabeth Street must have been built up substantially—probably when this was the main goldfields route—such that the Stork's original ground floor had been demoted to a basement.

Upstairs, in the years before it closed, the Stork offered old-style hotel accommodation—bed, chair, bare boards, bathroom down the hall—with the novelty of themed rooms. I stayed there once in the Kate Kelly Room, named in honour of the bushranger's sister. Folklore had it that members of the Kelly family had lodged at the Stork when they came to town in 1880 for Ned's execution. (See 4:M.)

7:D

HOLT'S MATRIMONIAL AGENCY
448 QUEEN STREET

On this spot used to stand a rather grand boom-time mansion: two storeys, triple-fronted, bay windows; columns flanking the entrance and concrete urns all along the fanfared parapet. It was built in 1894 by the Holts, Annie and James, as HQ of their matrimonial agency. For an upfront fee of one guinea, the agency sought life partners for men and women from all walks of life. If an introduction led to marriage, the Holts would be rewarded with, say, a fortnight's wages from a working man or, in the case of better-off clients, a percentage of the happy couple's combined fortune. The marriage-broking lark must have been a winner: the Holts were able to shell out £4,000 for their matrimonial chambers while the rest of Melbourne was mired deep in the 1890s depression.

Annie Holt had started in the marriage business around 1886. Before that she'd run a servants' registry and had noticed how often a widower would marry the housekeeper she found for him. Annie herself came from a broken home, with a ne'er-do-well father who threw his wife and children onto the streets, then shirked on paying maintenance. In James Holt, by contrast, Annie reckoned she'd found 'the best husband in the world'.

It was the 1892 trial of Frederick Deeming that made

Holt's Matrimonial Agency a household name. Deeming had written to Holt's seeking a new wife just days after murdering his old one. (See 1:M.) Not long after, the Holts had a windfall—a grateful client granted them the title to property she'd inherited in India—on the strength of which they built their palatial premises here.

'Opposite the old cemetery' may not sound like a felicitous locale, yet for fifteen years or more that phrase was fluted in daily newspaper adverts for Holt's. Up to 1905, the agency claimed credit for more than fifteen thousand marriages, many of them held on the premises. You see, in addition to its matchmaking service, Holt's Matrimonial Agency operated as Melbourne's Gretna Green. The Holts kept a roster of superannuated or discredited clergyman, so that there was always one available—from ten till ten, six days a week—to perform weddings without notice. The fee was ten shillings and sixpence, plus a few shillings more for ring and witnesses.

By law, a woman younger than twenty-one needed her parents' permission to marry, but it was never hard to persuade the Holts (who usually acted as witnesses) and their clergymen that the bride was older than she looked. Nor was it an obstacle to marriage if one or both parties were so drunk they could hardly stand up. Many a pair who'd only just met would end their evening's spree by getting spliced at Holt's and consummating their union in the old cemetery grounds. Not surprising then that the name of Holt's Matrimonial Agency came up frequently in court, both in cases of divorce and—more often—of bigamy. Having accepted a bigamist's defence that 'under the influence of drink [he] forgot his marriage vows', a jury acquitted him, only with a rider expressing their 'indignation that such agencies as Holt's should be allowed to exist'. The press decried the 'evils' of the agency, calling it 'a wholesale manufactory for illicit marriages'. And worse: 'There is a back door to Holt's that ought to be exposed.' Was there more to the marriage-broking business than met the eye—sinister doings in the cellar, run by a deep-state cabal? Luckily for the Holts, this was a hundred years before Twitter.

If there *was* a back door, it probably led to James Holt's workshop. When not witnessing harebrained nuptials, he practised and taught the trade of art metalwork, in particular *repoussé*: raised designs beaten into metal with hammers made of deer-antler. His main trade was ecclesiastical, supplying churches with chalices, pyx boxes, thuribles, vergers' staffs and the like. But he was also commissioned to create presentation pieces for military heroes, retiring lord mayors—even royalty. In 1889, as the colony of Victoria's silver-wedding gift to the Prince and Princess of Wales, he fashioned a pair of wine jugs with *repoussé* tableaux of First Australians hunting kangaroo against a background of fern fronds and gum trees. Each jug had a snake coiled around its lid, a handle in the shape of a climbing goanna—all exquisitely wrought in silver—and, forming the spout, a golden bird.

But James Holt's most notable creation—more lasting than the thousands of marriages solemnised in his and Annie's presence—must surely be the ceremonial mace, still used in Victorian parliament, that replaced the one stolen in 1891. (See 4:C.)

7:E

THE HOUSEWIFE'S BURDEN

MARKET TROLLEY HIRE, STRING BEAN ALLEY (M SHED)

The car-bell in that verse by Jonah (see 7:B) belonged to a tram car whose conductor persisted in announcing the market stop as 'God's acre'—the cemetery. And those go-carts and perambulators were improvised shopping trolleys. A go-cart was usually just a crate with wheels and broomstick handles but, right through to the 1940s, the market-shopper's favoured beast of burden and battering ram was a roomy old pram, preferably minus baby:

> *Babies being rather omnivorous creatures, many of them chew cabbage leaves, newspaper, or carrots as they are trundled along…and when the perambulator bangs and jerks over the cobblestones, their heads give an answering wobble, and as likely as not a piece of carrot jams in their throats.* (*Argus*, 1903)

Alternatively, there was the basket* or gunny sack and, later, string bags of miraculous capacity.

Boys with billycarts had a 'pitch' down by the market gates on Elizabeth Street, where they vied for the home-delivery trade. After World War Two, a campaign to reduce the housewife's burden (see 5:G) was backed by doctors, who warned of the dangers posed by 'shopping-bag neuritis'. At Victoria Market the *Argus* found and photographed 'a potential victim': a young woman juggling baby, suitcase, bulging string bag and bunch of gladioli.

Home delivery was one solution; another was the compact two-wheeled 'mobile shopper', pulled along by a handle. Better known (by me, anyway) as a jeep, it fitted neatly in a car boot or the aisle of a tram and by the late 1970s, when I first shopped there,† the Vic Market swarmed with them. Each was armed with a blunt metal prong—the stand that kept the jeep upright when stationary but which, on the move, stuck out behind. It was a lucky day at the market if you didn't gouge your shin on one.

* Economists relied on a notional 'market basket' to monitor consumer prices.

† My first outing to the market, one lunch hour, was to buy pecans for my boss. Tricky, since I didn't know what a pecan *was*.

7:F

FESTIVE FERN FROND FRENZY

MARKET CAR PARK ENTRANCE, QUEEN STREET

> *No other city in Australia is so partial to gum leaves as Melbourne, and at Christmas that partiality amounts to a mania.*

From its opening year, the Queen Vic Market on Christmas Eve was thronged with shoppers before daybreak, getting in their provisions for Christmas Day. The *Herald* called it 'one of the greatest sights of the Southern Hemisphere'. Live poultry had their feet tied with string that doubled as a carrying handle. Even more cumbersome and just as essential would be a monstrous sheaf of gum branches or fern fronds, the Melburnian equivalent of a Christmas tree:

> *To many thousands of dwellers in the city terraces, lanes and squares the Christmas market is the only opportunity of obtaining material for the bit of green garlanding which shall make the house gay.*

The mania began with a fad for fern-gully tourism in the 1870s, and lasted roughly fifty years. As late as 1921, fern fronds brought in by the cartload from the Dandenongs and beyond sold for sixpence a dozen at the Christmas market.* 'In every tram car that passed the markets, the passengers were tickled under the chin with fern fronds and gum leaves,' and it seems to have been a rare bystander who, at the sight of ambulating shrubberies, could resist invoking Birnam Wood and Dunsinane. But even in the early years, there were those who professed themselves aghast at 'the massacre of our forests' and 'this wholesale destruction of beauty spots' to garnish the city at Christmas time.

Up until the 1920s, there was something like a forest right next to the market. When the cemetery was first laid out, several stately old gums had been left standing. Removing their huge stumps was beyond the means of horsepower anyway, so why not keep the trees for shade? Graves nestled round them, even though the roots must have made hard work of digging. Then, after the cemetery was superseded in the 1850s, most of its trees fell victim to the firewood demands of the growing city.

Just one ancient tree—'as dead as anything there'—seems to have been suffered to remain as a kind of monument. It stood near this spot: on the Queen Street

* Also sold as Christmas ornamentation were bunches of pestiferous Scotch thistles, with which naughty boys would dart through the market, prodding and pricking female shoppers. *Larrikins are the weeds, the thistles and nettles of society…*

boundary, near where Franklin Street does its dog-leg.* Legend was that the huge old redgum had already been dead when Melbourne was founded and served as a landmark to venturers into the 'wilds' beyond the early township. Well into the 1880s, it stood out stark on the skyline—'atrociously beautiful' to one lover of the sublime *en route* to the university. A crowd of some hundreds gathered round the dead tree one afternoon in the spring of 1885, to watch as a man armed with a rifle and mounted on an upper branch eluded the police who'd come to arrest him. Eventually a constable climbed up and, after a scuffle, pulled the man down. Handcuffed and thrown in a cart, his screams caused the horse to bolt on the way to the lock-up.

At some point, even that last surviving tree was gone. But a species of rogue scrub—self-sown wattles and ti-trees, with lesser shrubs and weeds—made the untended cemetery grounds a wild counterpoint to the manicured Flagstaff Gardens nearby. Local kids loved this no-man's land, this scrap of urban bush. On Sundays, you'd see them carrying home armfuls of wattle blossom and greenery in rehearsal for the Christmas market.

* Plans for redeveloping the market include the straightening of Franklin Street, cutting it through the existing carpark and over the top of the old cemetery.

7:G

FLYING FISH

CORNER FRANKLIN & WILLIAM STREETS

During a lull in traffic one weekday morning in 1952, a large grey shag landed in the middle of this intersection and disgorged two live fish. A city-bound cyclist, without even dismounting, scooped up both fish and kept riding.

7:H

FLAGSTAFF HILL SUMMIT

FLAGSTAFF GARDENS (GRASSED PLATFORM OVERLOOKING KING STREET)

That Flagstaff Hill was once beyond the limits of Melbourne proper is clear from the siting of the settlement's first cemetery here. Five or six, or maybe more, graves were dug on the town-facing slope before the official cemetery (on the Vic Market site) opened for business. Then a fence was put around the little burying ground and, overlooking it, a signal station was built here on the hilltop. Burial Hill became Flagstaff Hill. The purpose of the flagstaff was to signal ships approaching and departing port. But the original flagpole turned out to be too short, so that signals had to be relayed via Williamstown. A taller pole, put up in 1841, incorporated a time-ball. In the absence of a public clock tower, a hollow metal ball was hoisted to the top of the flagstaff, then released—dropped—at noon each day, setting Melbourne mean time.

Shipping news was posted on a bulletin board at the flagstaff, and Melburnians awaiting cargo or letters or loved ones would visit daily. The many-windowed signal station also kept records of natural phenomena, including an earthquake in 1847 and, two years later, a snowstorm. In anticipation of news that the Separation Act of 1850 had been passed by the British parliament, plans were laid for a chain of hilltop beacon fires to kick off celebrations throughout the new colony of Victoria. A mighty bonfire on Flagstaff Hill, to be lit by the mayor of Melbourne, would give the signal to the rest. Someone beat the mayor to it, though, lighting the bonfire a day early and burning down the signal station's dunny into the bargain.

The arrival of the electric telegraph in 1854 made the signal station redundant. It became home, instead, to a magnetic observatory. With scientific instruments donated by the King of Bavaria, Georg Neumayer set out to survey terrestrial magnetism throughout Victoria, covering about ten thousand kilometres on foot and horseback. Such data would be useful for mineral exploration and geological mapping, and in assessing soil, groundwater and salinity. But the observatory on Flagstaff Hill was vital for testing Neumayer's theory of a correlation between changes in the earth's magnetic field and weather conditions. To conduct his research, he had a complex of 'magnetic rooms' built (using nails of brass and copper) around the old signal station. There was the sunken sixteen-sided Horary House, the Absolute House and a domed meridian room. Magnetic readings and meteorological observations were made on the hour, around the clock, by a roster of assistants that included William (Jack) Wills, the future explorer.

The iron crinoline hoops that gave loft to the skirts worn by a party of lady visitors to the Flagstaff Hill observatory in 1860 may have disturbed the delicate magnetic calibrations therein, and possibly contributed (it has been speculated) to the fatal disarray of the Burke and Wills expedition, which relied for direction on a combination of compass, dead-reckoning and camel-nav.* To be fair, the Flagstaff Hill observatory's sensitive instruments were thrown out too by the ironworks and tin roofs proliferating in the neighbourhood around that time.

Also disturbing Neumayer's readings was the gouging of a gravel quarry, for road-making, directly behind his observatory.† To let King Street pass through, the hill's western slope was blasted away, leaving a steep cliff on that side. The rest of the hill was progressively scraped bare, first of its trees for firewood, then of its topsoil for levelling streets and building sites throughout the city. By the end of 1850s, with Flagstaff Hill a dumping ground and an eyesore, local residents petitioned for it to be reclaimed as a public park that might, in time, be 'sufficiently beautified to become an ornament to the neighbourhood'.

They got their wish. By 1880 the hill was densely cloaked with trees which, over the years, would be thinned out and the parklands manicured with paths and ponds and monuments. Leaf blowers and statuary notwithstanding, the Flagstaff Gardens are recognised today as

* Neumayer, as part of his survey, accompanied the expedition as far as the Darling River.

† The observatory would eventually relocate to a more pristine locale south of the city.

a significant remnant of the Indigenous, pre-Melbourne landscape—a natural vantage point and gathering place, set back from the curving river, overlooking wetlands to the west and plains to the north and east.

7:1

ST JAMES'S OLD CATHEDRAL

VIEW FROM FLAGSTAFF GARDENS

A trick of topography and history makes the pepper-pot tower of St James's Old Cathedral float into view from Flagstaff Gardens as you approach the steps down the King Street escarpment. St James's was built in stages over a decade or more, from 1839, using iron-stained sandstone from a quarry on the south side of the Yarra, Melbourne's earliest source of building stone. Originally St James's Anglican *Church*, it became a cathedral when Melbourne was upgraded from town to city in 1848.

St James's used to stand at the corner of William and Collins streets, right in the heart of the early township. Over time, though, it lost its centrality and its congregation, until it was displaced as cathedral by St Paul's. As the church became leaky and its CBD site more valuable, St James's future was reimagined: it was pulled down in 1913—carefully unpicked, stone by stone—and reopened here on Batman Street the following year. Its bells, brought from London in 1852, were rung for the first time in years (the tower's decrepit old timbers had made it unsafe). They still ring every Sunday, and on Fridays for practice.

7:J

OLD CORNER SHOP

330 KING STREET (CORNER KING & LA TROBE)

The old shop-residence on this corner has had its side wall shored up by scaffolding for a few years now. Will it still be standing when you read this? Built in 1850, the year of the Separation bonfire on Flagstaff Hill, this humble corner store has been rattled half to bits by the relentless King Street traffic, and burdened on top of that with the weight of heritage. Only in recent decades has it been recognised as a rare survivor of pre-gold-rush Melbourne, to be hung on to at all costs. But the costs are high, and who's to meet them?

There are two sides to the heritage imperative: preservation of the old and prevention of the new—in particular, of yet another glass stiffy on a prime city corner. Surely the best argument for keeping old buildings in a modern city is one of scale, human scale. That, and the sense they convey of someone having been here before us.

I'm not talking about memory: memory can outlive

brick and stone. But the solid presence of old places, made and kept at human scale, gives a city and its inhabitants their bearings across time. Lose that and your city's a machine.

7:K

EAGLE ALLEY

OFF LA TROBE STREET

The big old oak that fills the tiny backyard of 330 King Street seems to yearn towards the Flagstaff Gardens. Originally a furtive dog-leg, Eagle Alley has borne its fair share of bloodshed, squalor and industry. Now it's been reconfigured, for parking access, into a crooked Y-shape. Follow the bend to where it meets the throughway linking La Trobe Street and Little Lonsdale. In one direction the view gives you a slice of the city; in the other a cut-out entry way frames the green tilt of Flagstaff Hill like a postcard, with the sweet visual pun of a speed hump sign in the foreground.

So, what's special about this unsung spot? Nothing. As far as I know.

INDEX